Teach Yourself VISUALLY™

Dog Training

Visual®

by Sarah Hodgson

WILEY

Wiley Publishing, Inc.

Library of Congress Control Number: 2005939197

ISBN-13: 978-0-471-74989-9
ISBN-10: 0-471-74989-3

Printed in the United States of America

10 9 8 7 6 5 4 3 2 1

Book production by Wiley Publishing, Inc. Composition Services

Praise for the Teach Yourself VISUALLY Series

I just had to let you and your company know how great I think your books are. I just purchased my third Visual book (my first two are dog-eared now!) and, once again, your product has surpassed my expectations. The expertise, thought, and effort that go into each book are obvious, and I sincerely appreciate your efforts. Keep up the wonderful work!

—Tracey Moore (Memphis, TN)

I have several books from the Visual series and have always found them to be valuable resources.

—Stephen P. Miller (Ballston Spa, NY)

Thank you for the wonderful books you produce. It wasn't until I was an adult that I discovered how I learn—visually. Although a few publishers out there claim to present the material visually, nothing compares to Visual books. I love the simple layout. Everything is easy to follow. And I understand the material! You really know the way I think and learn. Thanks so much!

—Stacey Han (Avondale, AZ)

Like a lot of other people, I understand things best when I see them visually. Your books really make learning easy and life more fun.

—John T. Frey (Cadillac, MI)

I am an avid fan of your Visual books. If I need to learn anything, I just buy one of your books and learn the topic in no time. Wonders! I have even trained my friends to give me Visual books as gifts.

—Illona Bergstrom (Aventura, FL)

I write to extend my thanks and appreciation for your books. They are clear, easy to follow, and straight to the point. Keep up the good work! I bought several of your books and they are just right! No regrets! I will always buy your books because they are the best.

—Seward Kollie (Dakar, Senegal)

Credits

Acquisitions Editor
Pam Mourouzis

Project Editor
Jennifer Connolly

Copy Editor
Ruth Strother

Editorial Manager
Christina Stambaugh

Publisher
Cindy Kitchel

Vice President and Executive Publisher
Kathy Nebenhaus

Interior Design
Kathie Rickard
Elizabeth Brooks

Cover Design
José Almaguer

Interior Photography
Jodi Buren

About the Author

Sarah Hodgson has been a trainer of dogs and their people for over 20 years. She has had many famous clients, including TV personality Katie Couric; actors Richard Gere, Glenn Close, Chazz Palminteri, Chevy Chase, and Lucie Arnez; business moguls George Soros, Tommy Hilfiger, Tommy Mottola, and Michael Fuchs; and sports greats Bobby Valentine and Alan Houston. She is the author of eight dog-training books, including *Puppies For Dummies*®, *DogPerfect*, and *PuppyPerfect*, and has two additional titles soon to be released: *Miss Sarah's Guide to Etiquette for Dogs and Their People* (2006) and *Dog Psychology For Dummies*®
(2007). Sarah lives in Katonah, New York, with her daughter, Lindsay, and her black Lab, Whoopsie Daisy. For more information, you can visit her website: www.dogperfect.com.

Acknowledgments

As always, there are so many people to thank—from the head of the dog to the tail that wags it. Pam Mourouzis, you are an inspiration to write for. Handing me off to Jenn Connolly was a great move—thank you. I don't know if it was more enjoyable to haggle over text or what to do about our children's teething and tantrums. Jenn—you are a joy to work with.

Jodi and Laurie—my photographers: although not one of these photos will hang in a gallery, each is indispensable for the people who are learning from them. That's the great accomplishment. Thank you for your tireless efforts! The week-long shoot is another in our memory bank.

On the home team, friends and family are the fur that warm and surround me. I could not have juggled the demands of this year and gotten this book out without all of you. Rosiemarie, Nancy, Sheila, Roma, Glen, Aunt Carolyn and Uncle John, Nona, LB and Dan, my entire church community—your support and love is all I really need in this world.

A GREAT big thanks to all my clients (both people and dogs) who hung out at the photo shoots day after day to bring the body of this work together. It was fun to have you all surrounding me while the stress of each shot was pending. My memories are great.

And finally to the tail that wags this dog—my Lindsay and the Whoops. You warm my heart and keep it beating. Love to all!

Table of Contents

chapter 3 Training Tools 26

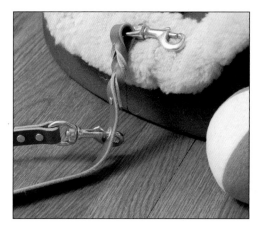

chapter 4 Proofing and Prevention 46

chapter 5   Puppy Kindergarten: Early Conditioning   62

chapter 6   Grade-School Lessons   76

chapter 7   The Invisible Leash   108

chapter 8   Socialization Plus   128

chapter 9 Games and Tricks 144

chapter 10 The Civilized Companion 164

chapter 11 Crisis Management 180

appendix A Choosing the Right Breed   202

appendix B Finding the Right Professionals   210

appendix C Everyday Care and Concerns 216

appendix D Kids and Dogs—from Coming Home to Everyday Living 226

1

Your Dog's Worldview

Before you jump into training your dog and strengthening your relationship, it is important to understand exactly what motivates your dog's happiness. Understanding how your dog thinks, views your home, and communicates with you is possible once you look at the world from your dog's perspective. The impulses that relate him to a breed (or a mix of breeds), his personality, and his energy level are all aspects of your dog that will shape his worldview and his association to you.

Your first step is to develop a game plan, a roadmap to help you organize each day and deal with frustrations that arise. A consistent plan that combines training exercises and daily structure will make the most sense to your dog. If your technique is inconsistent, your schedule fluctuates, you're absent for long periods, or your reactions to your dog are harsh and overwhelming, your dog's behavior will suffer. A dog does not misbehave when he feels safe, understood, and directed. Learning about your dog from the paws up is the first step in creating a lifelong bond.

Dogs Have Personality, Too

Every dog is unique, regardless of breed. Like a child, your dog needs to be loved for who he is, and you need to keep this in mind as you train him. You can't train every dog or puppy the same way—each one learns differently based on identifiable personality traits as well as breed characteristics. Here are six different personality descriptions. Consider where your dog fits in.

BOSSY

These dogs take themselves very seriously. Strong-willed and determined, they simply ignore anyone they don't respect. A dog with this personality requires a strong, consistent training program and is happiest when everyone involved takes the same approach.

COMEDIAN

These jokesters are always dancing on the edge of good behavior and will reveal any inconsistency within your approach or within the family. Engaging, they thrive on interaction and may be naughty simply to get attention. A comedian needs clear direction, consistent follow-through, and a calm approach. Being too stern can backfire as this dog will get hyper when a lesson becomes too rigid.

JOE COOL

This easygoing lot takes life in stride and may not pay attention to your concern, energy, or disapproval. These dogs often prefer to nap during lessons and can be challenging to motivate. Be persistent with your lessons; left undirected they can easily get distracted and find themselves in harm's way.

EAGER TO PLEASE

Dogs with this personality put your approval high on their priority list. The drive for attention is so great that these dogs may indirectly learn such routines as jumping up when greeting to get attention that don't meet with everyone's approval. Training need only be presented and reinforced in a consistent manner for this dog to cooperate.

SWEET PEA

These endearing dogs are gentle and loving, often preferring to view life from the sidelines. They prefer not to make waves and can sometimes appear overwhelmed if lessons are too strict. Adoring and sweet, they can be needy if ignored. A calm, praise-heavy training approach works best to bring out the best in this personality type.

TIMID

Dogs in this group do not tolerate new situations, dogs, or people well. Calm familiarity is reassuring to them. To an outsider, a timid dog may appear abused, as he cowers and hides at the slightest distraction. Consistent, affirmative lessons will help this dog establish a stronger sense of himself.

To determine a dog's or puppy's personality, you can do a series of exercises. Test A is best done on a puppy under 5 months; Test B is for dogs over 5 months.

Test A: Puppies Under 5 Months

1. Watch your puppy interact with other puppies. Is he

- **a.** Bossy, biting and climbing on the others' backs?
- **b.** Playful, responding to the others' interactions or carrying toys?
- **c.** More interested in you?
- **d.** Laid-back and relaxed?
- **e.** Content to sit alone?
- **f.** Fearful?

2. Cradle your puppy in your arms (if you can). Does he

- **a.** Squirm and bite to be freed?
- **b.** Mouth playfully, then relax?
- **c.** Relax immediately and lick your hand?
- **d.** Relax and look content?
- **e.** Look submissive, licking your hand with his ears back?
- **f.** Look afraid?

3. Shake a set of keys above your puppy's head without his knowing it. Does he

- **a.** Respond assertively, jumping up to bite the keys?
- **b.** Try to play with the keys?
- **c.** Look to you?
- **d.** React calmly?
- **e.** Look confused?
- **f.** Act fearful—tail tucked, ears back, hunched down?

4. Gently grasp the scruff of your puppy's neck, just behind his ears. Does he

- **a.** Turn to defend himself?
- **b.** Lay his ears back and reach up to playfully interact?
- **c.** Quickly lower himself to the floor and roll to one side playfully or lick your hand?
- **d.** Relax?
- **e.** Roll submissively to one side, and possibly pee?
- **f.** Look frightened—roll to one side, tail tucked under belly, ears pinned back?

5. Fall to the floor and pretend to grasp your knee in pain. Does he

- **a.** Pounce and bite you?
- **b.** Playfully run to you with his tail wagging?
- **c.** Run to you, putting his head under your body?
- **d.** Not respond?
- **e.** Act confused?
- **f.** Run to a corner, tail and ears down?

CONTINUED ON NEXT PAGE

Test B: Puppies Over 5 Months and Adult Dogs

1. **Call your dog in an enclosed space. Does he**
   a. Completely ignore you?
   b. Look and consider, perhaps staying just out of reach?
   c. Race right over or make a game out of keep-away?
   d. Slowly come or allow you to approach?
   e. Come quickly with a lowered posture signaling submission (if he left your side in the first place)?
   f. Get skittish?

2. **Approach your dog while he is chewing or playing with a toy. Does he**
   a. Protect the toy with a stiffened body?
   b. Playfully move his head so the object is just out of reach or tug to keep the toy?
   c. Welcome your approach or play a familiar game of keep away or tug?
   d. Lay his head over the toy or give the toy up without a struggle?
   e. Give the toy up while licking your hand or wagging his tail submissively?
   f. Look as if you're about to hit him or race away with the object fearfully and stay just out of reach?

3. **Wake your dog from a nap (clap your hands above his head). Does he**
   a. Jump up aggressively?
   b. Wake quickly and prepare to play or look for a toy?
   c. Get up and come to you?
   d. Only partially get up?
   e. Look confused and either come to you or move to a safe place away from the noise?
   f. Jump up and look frightened?

4. **Take a box of cereal to your dog's level and give him one treat at a time. Does he**
   a. Demand the box?
   b. Take the treat and playfully try to stick his nose in the box?
   c. Take one treat at a time, following your hand as you reach in for the next treat?
   d. Take the treat or, if hungry, nose the box?
   e. Take the treats one at a time?
   f. Take the treat quickly or take it and go to the box for more with a look of panic?

5. **Fall to the floor and pretend to grasp your knee in pain. Does he**
   a. Approach you and sniff?
   b. Playfully run to you with his tail wagging?
   c. Run to you, putting his head under your body?
   d. Not respond?
   e. Act confused?
   f. Approach you momentarily and then pace the room?

Interpret the Results

The answers to these questions will help you assess the puppy's or dog's personality.

- **Mostly A's: Bossy.** A dog who tries to control or dominate situations, is headstrong and self-assured, may challenge directions, and submits only to a consistent approach

- **Mostly B's: Comedian.** A playful dog who puts fun above obedience

- **Mostly C's: Eager to Please.** A dog who seeks your approval and is dependent on your interactions

- **Mostly D's: Joe Cool.** A laid-back dog who always approaches life in that manner. Although it sounds dreamy, it can be frustrating if you crave inter-action or involvement.

- **Mostly E's: Sweet Pea.** A reserved dog who is cautious and depends on direction

- **Mostly F's: Timid.** A timid dog who may let his fears override his trust if not worked with consistently

Few dogs get straight scores. Like human beings, they are a mix of traits.

Get a Proper Education

If you find that you need training help beyond the scope of this book, finding a training school or private trainer can be one of the best investments you'll make. Look for an individual who shows compassion for both you and your dog—someone who responds openly to your questions on everything from potty training to leash walking.

Find Additional Training Help

PRIVATE INSTRUCTION

It is important to like and agree with the person you choose to help you handle your dog. There are many good dog trainers, but finding an individual who can teach *you* is just as important. Here are a few questions to help you pinpoint your search:

- How long have you been in this business?
- May I speak to someone regarding your techniques?
- What books or websites do you recommend?
- How do you discipline a dog?
- What is your experience with my breed (or with shelter dogs or mixed breeds)?

It's best to find someone who is willing to answer these questions openly. A good trainer is usually busy helping dogs, so be respectful of her time: wait to ask for specific advice about your dog until you meet her face to face.

GROUP CLASS

Look for a class with six to eight dogs that groups dogs by age and ability. If you have a puppy, enroll him in a puppy kindergarten class. It is good for socialization. Ask if the class allows for off-leash playtime, and if you have a smaller breed, ask if there is a separate room or area for your dog to play in.

If your older dog is afraid or aggressive toward other dogs or has an extreme issue such as excessive barking, ask how the instructor deals with that situation. Also inquire if the instructor uses a specific training collar. In my classes, I offer a choice of five collars, since each dog is unique and needs specific equipment to help him learn. Finally, ask about the instructive philosophy for discipline—does the teacher discipline dogs in class?

When asking these questions, ask yourself if you are comfortable with this person and her answers. If you're not, look for other groups; you have choices.

chapter 2

Learning to Speak Doglish

When training your dog, it's important to look at the world from her perspective. She simply can't understand your world or your interactions as another human being would. In fact, your dog thinks of you and your family as other dogs in her pack. Understanding her way of communicating and how she learns and views your interactions is the topic of this chapter.

Understand Pack Theory

Before you can train your dog to listen to you, you need to understand just what makes her tick. Although you may not look like a dog, your dog responds and respects you as though you were. Straight down the canine ancestral line, dogs habituate behavior that is reflective of pack theory: where one is the leader and the others respect the leader's direction. Training is based on this instinct.

Who's in Charge

Long ago, dogs were domesticated from the wolf, and many of their social instincts remain the same. Wolves live in packs in which the social structure and hierarchy are predetermined and respected. Every pack has a leader who is responsible for everyone. This is a big job that can fall to either a male or a female. That leader and his or her partner together make up what is called the *alpha pair*.

When you bring a dog into your home, she is primarily interested in establishing who is in charge. This is why training your dog is so important for both of you. Most dogs prefer the relaxed role of a follower, but if you don't take charge, the dog will.

Dogs who are in charge typically exhibit a few to all of the following behaviors:

- Bark or paw at you for attention or a treat.
- Ignore you or run away when you say COME.
- Are unruly with company.
- Go to the bathroom in forbidden spots.
- Pull you on the leash.

These behaviors are not signs of a "bad" dog; they simply show a dog who thinks she is supposed to make decisions and be the leader.

Your dog's behavior is chiefly motivated by your attention. Relating to you is the highlight of her day, and she will do anything to get you to notice her, even if it's acting up.

Attention Is Everything

You dog thrives on your attention; she doesn't care whether it is negative or positive. In fact, negative attention is often perceived as confrontational play or, worse, instills fear. For example, it you yell loudly enough at anyone, they will look afraid. The same is true of your dog. You may be yelling at your dog, telling her that she's bad and thinking that she understands that you're mad at her. In reality, your dog may be misinterpreting your frustration and not making the connection. Your dog may be reading your frustration as confrontational play, making her even more excited and unmanageable.

Consider what I call the Attention Scale, a scale ranging from 1 to 10, with 1 representing sleep and 10 representing totally out-of-hand behavior. For our discussion we will further split the scale into 1 to 8, or the happy, civilized zone, and 8 to 10, the manic zone in which your dog literally can't control herself. As puppies, all dogs have this range; however, as they mature, most learn how to contain their impulses.

A lot of people focus on behaviors that fall in the 8-to-10 zone, manic impulsive activities, in an anxious attempt to gain quick control. Yelling, pushing, kneeing, and grabbing, however, are all forms of attention, but instead of teaching the dog to be calm, these reactions excite her, and the behavior gets worse or happens more frequently. Remember, the behavior that gets the most attention is the behavior that your dog will repeat over and over. Your goal is to help your dog understand how to control her own impulses and to live in the 1-to-8 zone: civilized and polite.

Play on the Same Team

Whether you're starting this book with a young puppy or an older dog with pre-established habits, think of this training adventure as a team effort. Your dog is the newest member of your team. She will learn your rules and expectations, provided that you can communicate them in a way she can understand.

Being a Captain You'd Respect

You must be the captain of your team. As the captain, you need to organize your dog's space and activities. She needs to know what she is supposed to do with herself in every situation, from where to go to the bathroom and what to chew to how to compose herself during the dinner hour and while you're entertaining company. Take a minute to think back to a team captain or coach that you admired. Now be that sort of leader for you dog. Come to your dog with a plan, communicate it consistently (i.e. where to go and what to do in all situations), and have patience for times when your dog is confused or acting up. Nobody's perfect: You're the captain so it's your job to teach and stay cool!

TIP

There are times you'll feel frustrated and maybe even angry at your dog. The hardest thing to control in fact, won't be your dog — it will be your temper. Outbursts, however, do more harm than good: they either frighten or excite a dog, with little or no long-term learning. Use the problem solving techniques listed throughout the book, consider leaving your dog on-leash when supervised to give you something to hold, or consider calmly placing her in a quiet area with a bone until you both cool off.

Think back to a team or group you've been involved with. Did you like your instructor or team leader? Did this person criticize you or make you feel good about your efforts? As your dog's team captain, always be the kind of leader you would want to follow.

Use the 5:1 Ratio

Consider your life from your dog's perspective, and be patient as you train her. She doesn't understand the difference between a stick and a wooden chair leg. She may think that it is her job to protect against intruders, even when the "intruder" is a visiting relative. She may be genuinely excited when she sees another dog approaching, although she's pulling you off your feet. Think about how she might be seeing things and use the exercises in this book to train her toward a better way of reacting.

A good team leader encourages more than discourages. Aim for a 5:1 ratio—say GOOD DOG five times for each NO you say. By focusing on good behavior, you make your dog feel good about herself, and she will cooperate more. Throughout this book's lessons, you will use food and toys to motivate your dog early on, but never let these rewards take the place of praise, both verbal and physical!

TIP

It is important to say your commands once, not repetitively: Repeating a command to your dog is confusing and delays understanding. Repeating a direction like COME or SIT would be like hearing someone ask you, "PLEASE PASS THE KETCHUP, KETCHUP, KETCHUP."

Learn to Interpret Doglish

Your dog's language—let's call it Doglish—does not consist of thoughts, statements, reasoning, or contemplation. Doglish consists of momentary choices and quick interpretations. Your dog relies on three vehicles for communication: eye contact, body language, and tone.

Eye Contact

Similar to human beings, dogs naturally look to their leaders for direction. The leader of the group is always kept within sight.

The first question to ask yourself is: are you looking to your dog more than she is looking to you? If so, your dog may be interpreting your attention as a need for leadership. During the next 24 hours, write down all the times you catch yourself looking at your dog.

Your dog is focused on your face most of the time. She knows when you look at her and will remember how to get your attention. If you look at her when she is behaving well, she's likely to repeat those positive behaviors.

Remember the phrase "You get what you look at." Focus on your dog when she is behaving well.

Body Language

Your dog responds to body language a lot like you do. A calm, confident posture reflects confidence and demands respect. A bent, lowered posture conveys either fear or insecurity. Frantic flailing conveys chaos or play.

When you're with your dog, make sure that your body language reflects your intentions. If you are training or trying to control her, stand tall and relaxed. Your dog will respect you if you maintain your dignity.

Note: If you have children, teach them to stand tall when giving the dog directions. Upright positions are confident poses; bending over is often perceived as playful. Refer to this posture as the Peacock Position for easy reference.

If you're playing with your dog or snuggling affectionately, you may get down to your dog's level. If she gets too excited or starts to mouth you in play, however, stand upright to remind your dog of your size and presence.

In addition to your posture, your dog is aware of where you stand in relation to her. If you're in front, you're the leader. If you are standing behind, you are seen as the follower. Take notice of this when your dog is excited or you're walking her in an unfamiliar area. If you are ahead of her, she will be calmer: you're in the position of leader, guardian, and protector. If not, she will naturally assume that role and may become aggressive or hyper.

CONTINUED ON NEXT PAGE

Tone

Dogs use the sound of their voices to communicate. A high-pitched whine signals intimacy or fear, a flat bark is directional, and a loud growl or bark is often a warning or an invitation to play.

Similarly, your dog responds to the tone of *your* voice. Confident directional sounds will get her attention and get her in the habit of looking to you for direction. Think of your commands as short, quick, directional barks.

Soft, loving tones and high-pitched squeals are best used to reward your dog rather than direct her. Dogs translate high-pitched or excited tones as play tones or fearful whimpers. Save these tones for play periods or loving attention.

Yelling is like barking to a dog. It is uncommon for one dog to charge another and bark repetitively in her face unless the dog is psychotic. It is especially confusing when you do it, since you are the person your dog wants to turn to when she feels threatened. Don't yell at your dog. It will not help in training her or strengthening your relationship. Many dogs look afraid when shouted at, but this is not understanding; it is fear.

Your dog responds to the tone of your voice, not to the actual words. Once you repeat a command many times, she will respond to the sound of the word and understand how to react when she hears it.

The direction of your voice is also important. If you stare at your dog and give her commands repetitively, she may feel overwhelmed. When your dog is exercising or playing, she won't be watching you so closely. When you give commands, either turn your body in the opposite direction or tilt your head upward. This will pique her curiosity, and she will look to you faster.

Dog-to-Dog Interactions

For a quick lesson in Doglish, watch two dogs together, preferably around the same age. If they are already friends, they will have a preestablished pattern of play and interaction. If they have not met, introduce them in neutral territory.

First, watch their eyes. Who is looking to whom? One should look to the other and follow her lead.

Next, check out their body language. Relaxed poses say that all is well. If the dogs are tense, it is because they are trying to determine who should be in charge. The one who rolls over or crouches is saying, "You can be the leader." This is known as a submissive posture. Notice that the leader dog often puts her head or paws on top of the other's back.

Some dogs are more vocal than others. Assertive growls and barks are another way to convey leadership, whereas playful yelps call out submission. Short, quick barks are often directional.

Read Your Dog's Postures

Learning to read your dog's postures may be easier than controlling your own. When trying to understand what your dog is experiencing, look to her ears, tail, mouth, body posture, and eyes.

EARS

- Rigid forward pitch = assertive, assertive and dominant posture
- Flat back = extreme fear
- Moving back to front = aware of surrounding sounds
- Angled back = submission, invitation to play
- Hanging loosely = relaxed

TAIL

- Arched high above the back = high alert, dominance
- Tucked under belly = fear, submission
- Just above rear end = alert but open and friendly
- Low carriage = cautious, submissive
- Fast wag above back = stimulated, dominant, preparing for a challenge
- Low wag between legs = Extreme fear, submission
- Sweeping wag just above rear end = open and friendly, curious and accepting

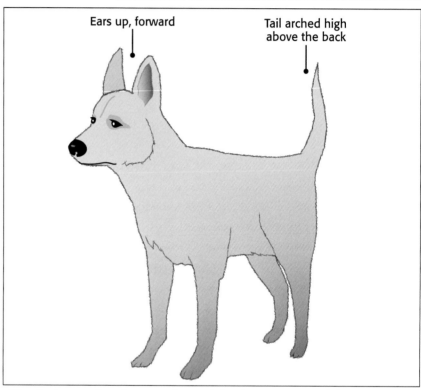

Ears up, forward

Tail arched high above the back

The dog's ears show her assertive and dominant posture, while her tail position illustrates her dominance and indicates that she's on high alert.

MOUTH

- Set jaw = snarl or sneer
- Lips pulled back = submission or fear
- Open face pant = welcoming, laughter, play
- Toothy grin = smile

EYES

- Direct stare = challenge, dominance
- Averted glance = submission or cold shoulder
- Downward glance = submission

BODY POSTURES

- Stretch = relaxed
- Play bow = submissive and playful
- Weight shifted forward = dominant
- Weight shifted back = submissive
- Lifted hair on neck (called hackles) = aggressive or threatened
- A still, curled posture = passive submission
- Low, quickly wagging tail, lowered body = active submission
- Mounting = dominance
- Lifted paw = submission or an invitation to play

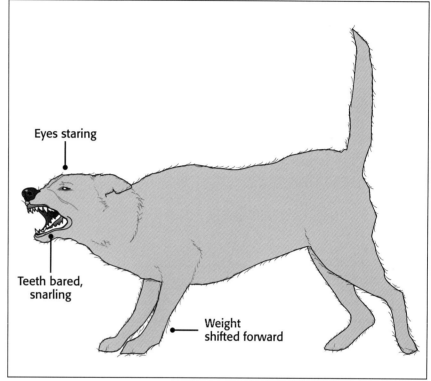

Eyes staring

Teeth bared, snarling

Weight shifted forward

The dog's jaw is set in a snarl, and her eyes are issuing a stare, indicating she's ready to challenge. Also note how her weight is shifted forward, showing a dominant posture.

Develop Sensory Awareness

Your dog depends on her five senses to understand what's going on around her. Understand this and you'll understand your dog a lot better. As you read, keep reminding yourself that no matter how much you love your dog—and no matter how much she loves you—she is not human. Her worldview is different. Understanding how she discovers and explores things will help you be a better teacher.

SMELL

Smell is your dog's strongest sense. It is many thousand times stronger than your own sense of smell. She depends on her nose to "see" what is around her. If you let your dog sniff a new object (like a brush, medicine, or a towel), she will be more comfortable with it. Also, let her sniff a new location, like your veterinarian's office or friend's home, before expecting her total attention.

SIGHT

Sight is not a dog's strongest sense. Dogs in general are nearsighted, seeing shapes and movements without distinction. However, your dog can see at night with nearly the same detail as her day vision.

Your dog will use her sense of smell to identify objects. When your dog sees an unfamiliar object, she may bark at it and seem cautious—she needs to smell it to feel comfortable with it.

Dogs are however, dependent on sight to interpret your interactions. Your dog will look to you for direction and focus on you when you give her a command.

Kneel down and look into your dog's eyes once a day with a warm stare. Wait until your dog looks away. If you meet a strange dog, don't look at it: doing so may signal a challenge, and she may attack you.

HEARING

Your dog hears much better than you do and can hear sounds that you can't. Her sense of hearing helps your dog keep a tab on what's happening around her. It may be quiet in your home, and then suddenly your dog barks furiously. She has heard something and is alerting to the intrusion. Although you can teach your dog not to bark at every sound or to quiet down, barking is a normal response to unusual sounds.

Your dog will rely on her ears to learn directions from you, too. Never scream at a dog, as it is perceived as barking. If you do yell, you may notice your dog barking back at you or looking frightened. It's like you're a stereo on full blast.

TOUCH

When you touch a dog, it is understood in one of three ways:

- As loving and nurturing
- As playful
- As an attack

Soft, loving pats will help calm your dog and put her at ease. Scratching or roughing her up will invite her to play, as she may think you're nipping her.

A dog's neck and throat are sensitive areas that can signal attack if grabbed suddenly or with force. If you pet a strange dog in either of these areas, she may think that you're challenging or going to attack her. Be careful.

TASTE

Your dog's sense of taste is very bland. She doesn't chew food; she tears and gulps it. She also doesn't digest food as well as we do. Keep her diet consistent. Don't leave chocolate out where your dog might get into it: it is a toxic poison that could kill her.

Your dog cannot taste or digest the many foods that humans can. Keep her diet consistent and avoid foods that contain sugar.

Understand Cause and Effect

Your dog will learn what behaviors to repeat based on what happens when she does them. If, for example, you push your dog off of you when she jumps, she will jump again, as dogs consider pushing to be rough play. On the other hand, if you hold a treat above her head, and when she jumps you lift the treat up and wait patiently until she sits before you reward her, she will learn to sit when she wants things. The same holds true for many other behaviors.

Control Your Dog's Reactions

If your dog is frantic at the door and is allowed to race outside, that is how she will act at all doors. You must learn to have her WAIT calmly at the door until she is released with an OKAY. She will have better door manners in the future.

Wrong behavior

Right behavior

Does your dog get hyper when she sees another dog? If you allow her to pull you over to the new dog and to greet her wildly, you will have no more control when your dog is off-leash. Instead, you must teach your dog to follow at your heel (HEEL) and to play when you give the release GO PLAY!

Right behavior

Can your children rile your dog into a frenzy of nipping and biting? The kids' fast motion and high-pitched squeals are very exciting. If you get angry, your dog will see you as just another participant in the fun. Instead, you need to repeat setups (see page 54) that will teach your dog how to contain her enthusiasm.

Wrong behavior

Right behavior

Does your dog steal objects to bait you into a game of catch? This is an age-old favorite. Your guaranteed participation is addictive. Instead, you must teach a release word like SHARE, and get your dog to bring you the object or to stand still while you retrieve them.

Wrong behavior

Right behavior

TIP

If you look at her when she's barking, jumping, has a shoe in her mouth, or is cruising the counter, she will repeat those negative behaviors to get your attention over and over again. It won't matter how angry you get at her, because dogs don't understand human frustration. Either they become defensive and aggressive over time, or they interpret the interaction as confrontational play or prize envy.

3

Training Tools

Every dog is different, and so is every home. What you and your dog will need depends a lot on your situation, the dog's age, and what works to help both of you learn best. In this chapter, you'll find descriptions of the safest equipment for training your dog. Remember, if one item is not working to simplify your situation, look for another option. Dogs were put on the earth to reduce stress, not elevate it!

Creative Confinements

Some dogs get restless when left alone or have trouble containing their bladder. A confined space can eliminate a lot of anxiety and limit their options to chewing or sleep. Eventually these habits will become ingrained, confined or not.

CRATE

A crate is a small pen for your dog to rest or sleep in—it is not big enough to play in or move around in. Although it looks and sounds confining, a crate is like a den for your dog. It helps him learn to rest when you're away or sleeping and aids in housetraining, as most dogs do not go to the bathroom where they sleep.

Crates come in many varieties, but your dog won't care what type of crate you use as long as you put his crate in a familiar spot. Always leave him a toy to play with or a bone to chew.

If you're going to crate your dog at night, consider putting the crate by your bedside. Your dog will be happiest and calmest when sleeping near you.

PLAYPEN

A dog's playpen is a segmented fold-out fence that provides an area large enough for your dog to move, play, and stretch in. It may be purchased in either plastic or wire. Its size varies depending on how many panels you attach together. A playpen is an ideal option if you are gone for long hours or for periods when you can't supervise your puppy's freedom.

If you do work long hours, place toys and bones in the pen, as well as a water dish. If you have a young puppy or a dog who you are paper training, you may also leave papers in one section of the pen.

When you return to your dog, do not pet or greet him until he is calm and either standing or sitting with all four paws on the floor. If you excite him, he may learn to tip the pen over.

GATES

Gates are a perfect way to enclose areas and still allow free play. There are many gates on the market, so consider the options as they relate to your dog. Pressure gates prop between two walls, and other gates can be secured into the wall with screws. These gates have doors that make it easier for you to move through them. Fortunately, there are wide gates and tall gates that accommodate any situation.

Dogs like to feel welcome and directed in each room and when they travel. A mat or bed can serve to direct them in your home and will be comforting when you visit or travel.

Mats/Beds

Give your dog a special place in each area of the house you spend time in so when he enters a room, he'll know where to go. Pick a location that is close to where you'll be in that room

Help your dog get organized by placing all his toys and chews on his mat/bed. When you want him to settle down on the mat, instruct him to SETTLE DOWN and chew his BONE. Pet him when he cooperates; secure him to his bed area with a leash if he won't settle down.

To decide which bed is best for your dog, consider what makes him feel comfortable; many dogs are happy with a flat mat, which is easy to wash and transport.

Help your dog with car travel by bringing along a favorite mat, or keep a special travel one in the car. This mat will help him identify his space. If you're going on an overnight trip, bring the bedding with you to help your dog behave. When going to the veterinarian, bring the mat to put on the table. Doing so will make it a more pleasant experience for everyone.

Dogs enjoy activities, especially when they're young and restless. Skip the crayons and handheld computers; however, purchase a few toys and bones instead. Not only do they entertain, but they also soothe the teething stage.

TOYS

There are many toys on the market for dogs. Some your dog will really enjoy; others he may rip to shreds or ignore completely. There are stuffed toys, rubber toys, ropes, squeak toys, Kong toys. Once you find a favorite type of toy, buy several and spread them around your home. Consistent toys will help your dog identify what is his.

If your dog rips a toy, throw it out immediately.

CHEWS

There are a wide variety of chew toys on the market as well. Some are made of animal parts that have been twisted and basted. Pet stores carry everything from pig ears to horse hooves. Many of these chews are odorous, so be sure to give them a sniff before you buy. There are also chews made of pulverized cornstarch, vegetable matter, and pig hide. Your dog will know what satisfies his urge to chew. Once you identify which object this is, buy it in bulk. Dried, hollowed-out bones are ideal for tucking peanut butter in, but some of them splinter, so supervise your dog's chewing until you're sure that the chews you have purchased are of good quality.

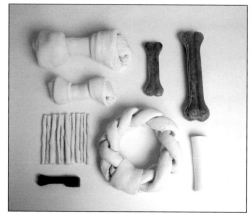

When training your dog it is helpful to have a collar or harness that he will wear when you're practicing. Depending on your choice the collar will either help you manage him without resistance, or issue a discouraging correction when he ignores your direction.

Your dog must wear identification tags whenever you leave the house. These tags should be placed on a buckle collar or harness. Do not place them on a training collar; not only would they weigh it down, but they could get caught and cause discomfort or choking.

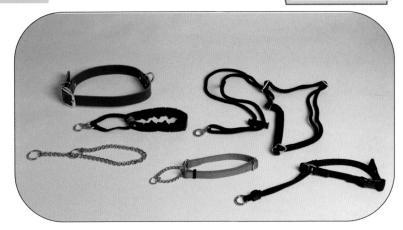

Fit a Collar or Harness

To measure your dog for a neck collar, take a tape measure and wrap it around his neck behind his ears (a).

To measure for a harness, measure across his chest and around his rib cage (b).

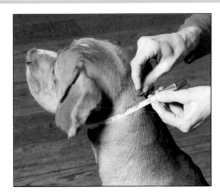

A properly fitted collar allows you to comfortably slide two fingers between your dog's neck and the collar. A snug but not tight fit is best.

Note: *If you purchase a leather collar or harness, watch for stretching over time, and secure it increasingly tightly if necessary to prevent slippage. If you purchase a collar or harness made of a nylon web material, the dye may bleed when wet. To prevent this problem, soak it in the sink overnight.*

You use a training collar when teaching your dog a new skill, such as walking on a leash or coming when called. Each type of training collar works differently; there is not one that is ideal for all dogs. The following descriptions will help you choose the one that is best suited for you and your dog.

To fit your dog for a training collar, measure the circumference of his neck, just behind the ears. Add two inches and purchase that length.

Types of Collars

TRADITIONAL CHAIN COLLAR

When used properly, a chain collar is very effective, although it takes some coordination and timing to make it work. It is the sound of the chain near your dog's ear that will teach him to avoid pulling, not his being choked. If you find yourself choking your dog when walking him on this collar, make another selection.

There is a right and a wrong way to put on a chain collar. If you put it on backwards, it can catch and hurt your dog. To put the collar on, first slide one end of the chain through the other loop. Next, make the letter P with the chain and slide it over your dog's head. The top ring should slide through, not bend over the other ring.

MARTINGALE OR CHECK CHAIN

This collar is three-quarters flat nylon mesh and one-quarter slip collar. The difference between a martingale and a check chain is that the martingale slip is made of nylon fabric and the check chain is one-quarter chain. The martingale and check chain collars are perfectly suited for long-necked breeds, like Greyhounds and Whippets, or calm dogs who simply need a gentle reminder to behave.

GOOD DOG COLLAR

This collar is a plastic, blunter version of the original prong collar. You can take it apart by unsnapping any of the links. Simply fold between any two links in an L shape and slide it out of the indented spaces. Position the collar so that the cord falls between your dog's ears. When the collar is attached to a leash, simply pull back on it to create a "scruff shake" feeling. A scruff shake is what dogs do to each other to clarify who is in charge. This collar can be used to discourage pulling, jumping, crotch sniffing, nipping, and more.

To fit your dog for a good dog collar, attach the collar around his neck and add or remove links until it's snug, but not tight.

NO-PULL HARNESS

This harness controls the leg muscles associated with pulling. It actually prevents your dog from pulling you. Although it sounds like an ideal option, it rarely teaches your dog to walk with you unless the harness is on.

To fit your dog, take measurements of his chest (across) and around his rib cage (diameter). Bring these measurements to a local pet store and ask for help choosing the no-pull harness that's best for you.

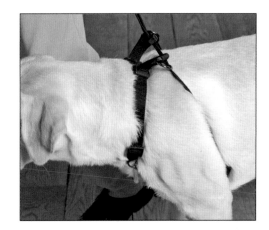

HEAD COLLAR

A head collar has a mellowing influence, as it lies atop your dog's nose and is secured on his neck behind his ears. These are two spots that dogs use to control one another, so a collar that puts pressure on those areas has value in calming dogs. Although a head collar looks like a muzzle, it works more like a halter on a horse. Without interfering with a dog's mouth, it enables a person who is less powerful than the dog to handle him with ease. It is a good choice when you're starting to train your dog, as it conditions good behavior almost immediately.

CONTINUED ON NEXT PAGE

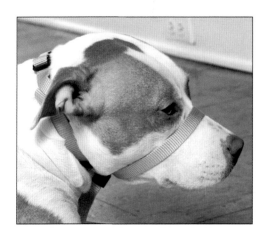

Putting on a Head Collar

1 With the collar in hand, clip the neck section directly behind your dog's ear and slide it so that it fits snugly. It should be watchband tight. Although it may seem too tight at first, when positioned, the strap will lie on your dog's jawbone and will not disrupt his breathing.

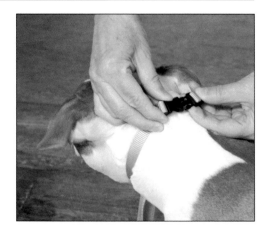

2 Unclip the neck strap and slide the nose loop over your dog's nose into place, bringing the clip up until the loop is positioned just behind the dog's lips. When the neck section is secured, the two together should make a V shape, not an L.

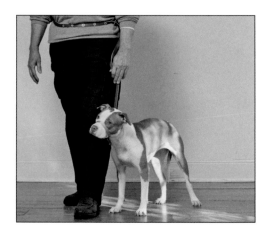

3 Let your dog get accustomed to wearing the head collar a few times a day for twenty minutes each time. He may scratch or rub his nose initially, like a child with new braces. Give him one to three days to get used to wearing the collar before clipping a leash to the ring located under his nose.

A leash, or lead, gives you the ability to direct your dog without grabbing for him. It is a calm way to teach him and its use will give friends and family a way to be consistent without physically handling him. Many leashes are available to you. The following descriptions tell you which leash is best to use in a given situation.

INDOOR DRAG LEAD

There are two drag leads that will help you teach your dog good manners and train him to respond to you. An indoor drag lead is a four-foot leash that attaches to your dog's buckle/tag collar or his Gentle Leader. You use it when advised to interrupt problem behavior calmly. It prevents you from having to chase or jump at your dog in order to catch him.

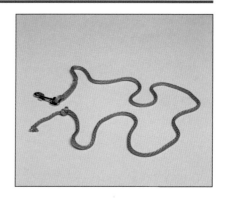

OUTDOOR DRAG LEAD

An outdoor drag lead is a twenty-five- to fifty-foot rope that attaches to your dog's buckle or tag collar. It enables distant corrections to problem behavior and aids you in teaching off-lead obedience. Purchase or make the lightest possible line so that it won't interfere with your dog's activities. A light cotton-nylon mesh is ideal: twenty-five feet for dogs under thirty pounds and fifty feet for large and fast-moving breeds.

This long line is an ideal tool for working on distance control, especially with the WAIT-OK, DOWN, and COME commands.

HAND LEAD

When secured to your dog's buckle collar, this short eight to twelve-inch leash reminds him that somebody is watching, while still giving him freedom to move about. A gentle reminder, the short attachment gives you the capacity to guide him subtly when his thoughts go astray. It can also be used for off-leash training exercises or secured to a seatbelt as a security system in the car.

CONTINUED ON NEXT PAGE

FINGER LEAD

Like a hand lead, this short two-inch loop attached to your dog's tag collar gives you easy access and quick control, especially for problem nipping and jumping.

RETRACTABLE LEASH

This leash is an ideal complement to working toward off-leash control and focus (see chapter 7). Once you accustom your dog to the pull of the retractable lead, it is ideal for reinforcing long-distance STAY and COME commands.

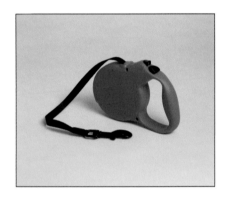

STATION LINE

This six- to ten-foot lead has a clip attached to either end. To use it outside, secure it to a tree or post and work on controlling your dog at a distance or helping him overcome separation anxiety.

Teaching your dog good containment skills is the first step in helping him learn to stay. This lesson does not come from correcting hyperactivity, but from rewarding and encouraging calm behavior. Although your dog may have trouble calming down initially, a few repetitions of being secured and praised for civil behavior is all he needs to understand what you want.

STATION LEAD

A two- to three-foot leash attached to the base of a piece of furniture or other immovable object will secure your dog in one area of a room and improve his understanding of the word STAY.

CARGO LEAD

A station lead can also be used to secure your dog in your car's back cargo area. It should provide just enough room for your dog to stand comfortably and lie down, but not enough room for him to climb over the seat.

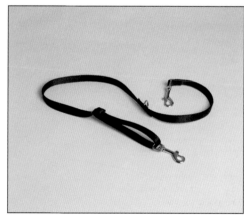

Teaching Lead

A teaching lead is more than a leash. It's a leash-belt combination that has five uses: it allows you to "wear your dog," providing a hands-free system of walking him; it enables you to hold your dog with a hand loop, providing him six feet of freedom; and it works as a short-station, a long-station, and a cargo-containment lead. Once you learn how to use a teaching lead, it will help you communicate with your dog all day long.

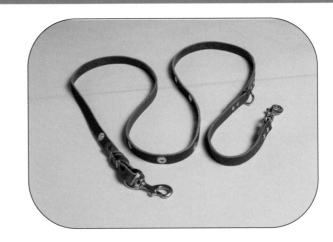

Introduce the Teaching Lead

To use the hands-free teaching lead system, put the training collar on your dog and then secure the leash around your waist as if it were a belt.

1. Begin walking in an open room, yard, or driveway.

2. If your dog walks ahead of you, simply turn away from him, say LET'S GO, and walk in the opposite direction. Do this several times until he is choosing to follow you.

Now you can teach your dog how to behave in the house without fearing that he'll bolt or get into mischief. You can also supervise his chewing, bathroom, and stealing habits. (See chapter 6 for more problem-solving ideas.)

3. As you walk through your home, give the leash a tug every once in a while to remind your dog to pay attention to you. If he's not cooperating, go back to step 1.

Use the Teaching Lead to Teach Station Stays

By stationing your dog to an object, you can teach him how to stay still. It's best to start doing this when you are in the room or nearby.

1 Select a spot at which to secure the leash, and put a bed there with toys on it for your dog to play with.

2 Take your dog to the bed, instruct him to SETTLE DOWN, and secure him with the leash.

3 Secure the end clip into the base hole to make the lead the shortest possible length.

4 If your dog can't sit still, stay close to him until he is more comfortable with being confined.

CONTINUED ON NEXT PAGE

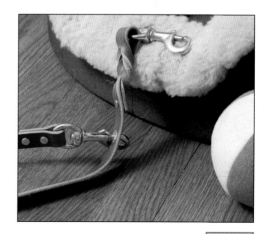

TRADITIONAL LEASH

There's a D ring on the teaching lead that you can use to secure one end clip to create a traditional six-foot leash. Once it's connected, there is no difference between a teaching lead and another kind of leash. This is ideal when it's time to let your dog go to the bathroom.

CAR CONTAINMENT

You can use the teaching lead to secure your dog to the head rest. Simply attach the clip to the end loop on the base ring and secure it around either object.

QUICK STATION

When you're out and about with your dog, you have a traveling station lead to allow you to secure him to a tree or table in a pinch.

Note: *Never leave your dog unattended in public. Ask someone to watch him if you are alone, and never lose sight of him.*

The project of housetraining your dog is straightforward once you decide on the location. A bell to alert you, material to highlight your dog's potty, and a solution to mask the scent of an accident are all extras that enhance both his understanding and communication.

BELLS

Get your dog to ring a bell when he must go outside to go to the bathroom. Hang a set of bells by the door at your dog's nose level. Each time you take him out, say OUTSIDE, stop at the door, and tap the bell with your fingertips. If after one week your dog is still not making the connection, lace the bell with a little peanut butter or yogurt ahead of time, and when you bring your dog up to the door, stop and see if he licks it. If not, show it to him. The moment he does lick it, open the door and take him outside.

You can also use a bell to teach your dog to signal to come in.

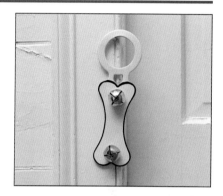

WEE-WEE PADS

If your goal is paper training, you'll need to designate specific areas in the main rooms you share with your dog. Eventually, you can phase down to one place, as outlined in chapter 10, but initially, you'll just need to help your dog understand that he must eliminate on a specified absorbent surface.

To this end, I recommend using white wee-wee pads and rolling up carpet until this habit is formed. You can purchase wee-wee pads through pet stores or catalogs, or in bulk at a pharmacy, where they are marketed as human incontinence pads.

NATURE'S MIRACLE

There are products on the market that can be used to mask the odor of a dog's housetraining accidents. It's important to eliminate this scent indoors, as dogs like to go to the bathroom in the same area repeatedly. Nature's Miracle is the name of the original solution, although your pet store may carry other effective products. A 50-percent mixture of vinegar and water also works well.

Several extras make the task of training your dog a fun and rewarding experience for both of you. These items will help you bridge the gap from confusion and chaos to understanding.

TREAT CUPS

There are several uses for a treat cup, all of which will increase your dog's enthusiasm for being with you. To make a treat cup, simply cut a hole in the lid of a container and fill the container halfway with your dog's food, dried cereal, or a favorite snack. Shake the cup and treat your dog ten times in a row to help him connect the sound of the cup shaking with getting a treat.

SNACK PACKS

You can use any generic fanny pack for this purpose. It is simply a hip bag filled with your dog's favorite treats/dry food. Wearing it gives you instant access to food rewards, and makes you your dog's focal point. Your dog will return to you and do whatever behavior gets you to open that pouch! In turn, this lets you select the behavior you want your dog to repeat, while eliminating the rest by simply ignoring him. For example, if your goal is to have your dog sit when he wants a treat or attention, ignore every other behavior he might offer you such as pawing, whining, jumping, or barking. Simply pretend he's not there until he sits politely. Then treat!

SPRAY-AWAY SHOOTERS

Spray-away shooters are meant to startle your dog, but they are not meant to be seen as coming from you. They are useful in correcting nipping, jumping, barking, stealing, and chewing habits. It is important not to spray your dog in the face angrily. Instead, hide the sprayer in your hand so that your dog won't see it, and spray his legs or torso from behind him so he won't know it's coming from you. The three top rated shooters are:

BITTER APPLE

This distasteful solution can be sprayed on objects and clothing to deter nipping and chewing. Place several bottles around your home and spritz objects/people calmly as your dog is chewing/biting them. He will choose to stop chewing these objects/people on his own. In this instance it is not necessary to hide the bottle from your dog, but avoid getting involved. It is simply a cause-and-effect correction that he will learn from on his own.

BREATH SPRAY

A small canister of breath spray fits neatly into a pocket or fanny pack and can be sprayed to deter mouthing or jumping. Never spray your dog in the face or eyes. Simply spray what he is biting, nipping, or jumping toward.

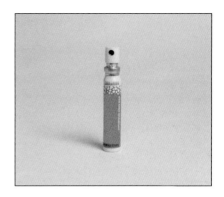

DIRECT STOP

This canister of citronella is more powerful than breath spray and can serve to startle your dog when he is barking or jumping on company, furniture, or counters. You do not want him to see you spraying him. Do it from behind as detailed in the section, "Spray-away Shooters."

Clicker Training

A clicker is a hand-held object that makes a sharp sound when you depress its metal strip. The distinct sound captures your dog's attention. The objective is to pair the sound of the clicker with a food reward. If your dog is not food-motivated, you can use a toy or a quick burst of attention to help him learn that the click is a positive sound. Food rewards are ideal so make the incentive strong. If your dog will work harder for a piece of meat than cereal, use it.

Introduce the Clicker

When doing the following exercise, do not speak. Let your dog focus on the noise of the clicker alone.

1 Line up ten bits of food. Your dog should be able to swallow each bit within two seconds.

2 Place the clicker behind your back or in your pocket, as the noise can be startling initially. Hold the treat in your other hand.

3 Click and treat in that order.

4 Finish the ten treats and end the interaction with attention or play.

5 Repeat the session until you can clearly see by your dog's enthusiasm and his expectation of the food after the clicker sounds that he has made the connection.

Think of your clicker as a camera photographing moments you want to see again. Use it to mark good behavior, such as when your dog goes to the bathroom in the right place, comes when he is called, or releases a toy when asked.

The clicker should not be used to encourage cooperation. If you want your dog to COME to you, for example, you use your clicker when he is at your side, not to get his attention.

Throughout the book, I will suggest ways to use a clicker or a word marker like YES to mark cooperative behavior. The word YES should be said sharply, like the sound of the clicker, and can help your dog understand exactly what is expected of him.

Here are three other ways that you may use the clicker or a word marker to help your dog understand what you're teaching him.

SIT

As you use the techniques on page 79 to teach your dog to sit, use the clicker to mark the exact moment he moves into position. Reward him instantly with food. Good dog!

STAND STILL FOR GREETINGS OR ATTENTION

Many dogs jump when greeting family or company. It is a normal impulse to want to get close to a person's face. With a clicker and food in hand, stand still and cover your face with folded arms if your dog is jumping at you (see chapter 11). When he stops and is calm, lower your arms, and then click and reward.

COME

Your first goal in chapter 6 will be to teach COME as a command of closeness. With your clicker and food in hand, say COME when your dog is near you. Encourage him to look up by sweeping your hands up to your eyes. Click and reward. Gradually extend the distance. Click and reward the instant your dog comes back to your side.

4

Proofing and Prevention

Because your dog really doesn't know what it is to be human, you might notice some extreme reactions when introducing her to your world. Although you may love your neighbor and every squeal of a young child, your dog may not agree until she's properly conditioned to them.

Many everyday sights and sounds can overwhelm a dog's senses. Your dog has more acute hearing than humans and can hear high-pitched sounds we can't register. Your dog also experiences sights far differently than you do. Our world is interpreted through vision—it is our strongest sense. Your dog, on the other hand, cannot distinguish color, relying on her vision only to interpret motion and posture. This is why many dogs react unfavorably to bikers, joggers, cars, and so on.

In this chapter, you will discover many creative ways to condition your dog to these and other distractions.

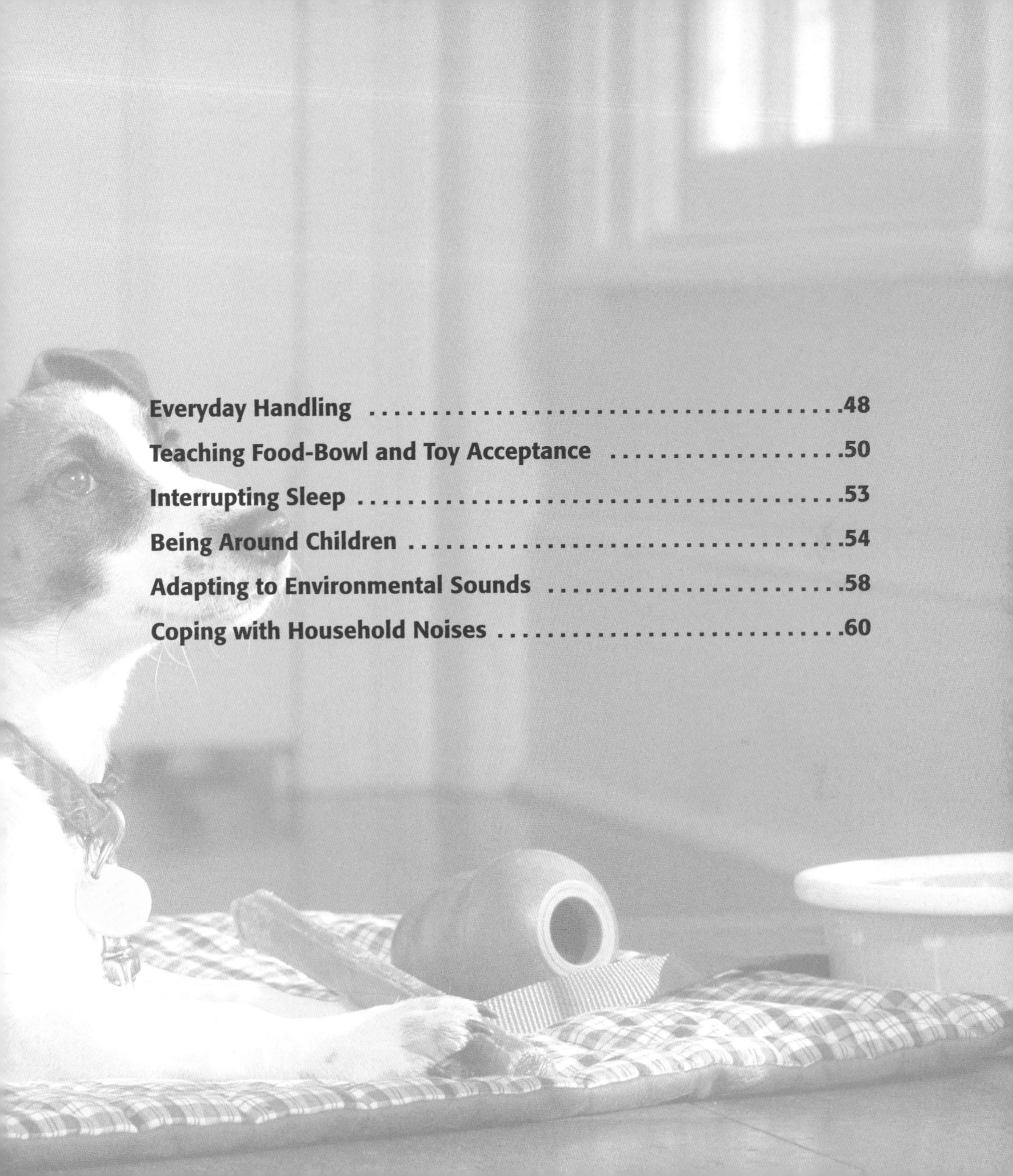

Everyday Handling

During her lifetime, your dog will experience many strange physical sensations, from her yearly checkups, with the veterinarian's prodding to determine illness or incident, to the unpredictable touch of a child. Since your dog can't verbalize pain, human handling is the only way to determine the source of her discomfort. Conditioning your dog to being handled is in everyone's best interests.

Handle Your Dog Daily

PAWS

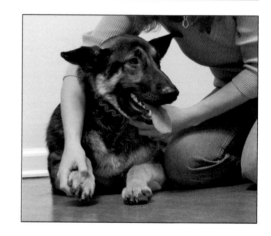

Each day, touch your dog's paws and toes. Feed her treats or let her lick butter of your hand as you touch each paw individually, running your fingers through along each toe. Doing this will help her accept examination and toenail clipping when necessity demands it.

If your dog resists, use treats, a creamy spread, or a favorite toy to distract her positively. If she bares her teeth, please call for professional assistance.

FACE

Soothingly caressing your dog's face is probably not something you need to be instructed to do, but there will be times—especially during your dog's yearly checkup or if she's agitated—when you or your veterinarian may need to handle her mouth, ears, or eyes. To prepare her, gently touch and probe her face in ways that her veterinarian handles her during an examination. Make this a part of your daily interactions so that your dog conditions to this handling as normal and loving.

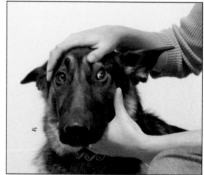

BELLY

Sometimes your dog's belly will need a little more than a scratch to determine if it's upset. Your veterinarian will probe your dog's belly as a matter of examination, so to prepare your dog for this unusual sensation, touch her underbelly gently with your index finger and thumb from time to time.

If your dog is particularly sensitive, treat her generously while you touch her tummy.

TAIL AND TUSH

Some breeds, commonly the Oriental breeds like Chow Chows and Lhasa Apsos, do not like being touched below the waist. Whether or not you experience this resistance, make tail and rear end pats a part of your daily handling. Gently scratching above your dog's tail and circling your fingers around her tail as you praise and treat her will ensure that she's comfortable being handled all over.

TIP

Many dogs are uncomfortable being medicated. To help your dog accept this reality of life, pretend to place drops in her ears, eyes, mouth, and so on without actually doing so. Give her treats as you're playacting. When the time comes, she'll be more comfortable with the procedure.

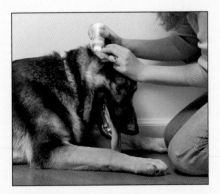

Teaching Food-Bowl and Toy Acceptance

Dogs are not born with an innate concept of sharing. Without specific conditioning and training, they will never acquire it. Although some dogs will submit to a person's interference while they're eating or chewing a toy, most consider the intervention a nuisance; some dogs even become aggressive.

It's important to teach your dog to share at as young an age as possible. Let your dog know that your arrival is not an attack and that you're there to congratulate her, not steal her prize.

Teaching Techniques

RECOGNIZE SPATIAL AGGRESSION

Dogs have five levels of aggression. The first two levels are

- Coveting—laying her head over the object;
- A short warning growl emanating from her throat.

By demonstrating aggression at these levels, your dog is letting you know that she does not want to be bothered and would prefer privacy when eating, chewing, or playing with an object—this is known as spatial aggression. She must learn to share if she is to live happily with people.

DISCOVER YOUR DOG'S RED ZONE

If your dog is showing any aggression, you need to determine her Red Zone: the closest distance you can stand to her before she gets uncomfortable. Let's say that when you're closer than three feet, she growls, but at three and a half feet she's comfortable. Less than three and a half feet is your dog's Red Zone.

Repeat the sequences described on the next page with the treat cup but stop, shake, treat, and reward just outside the zone. As your dog trusts your presence, slowly move closer.

TEACH YOUR DOG TO SHARE

As described on page 42, make treat cups and place them around your home. At any opportunity, approach your dog when she's with an object or food, shaking the cup. Offer her a handful of treats, praise her, and then walk away. Do not speak to, or interfere with, the object.

If your dog hesitates or seems unsettled by your approach, walk toward her sideways. Dogs view side postures as less threatening. If your dog shows more aggressive tendencies, see the previous page. Consult a professional if you are fearful or her reaction doesn't improve.

As your dog grows more familiar with your approach, she'll begin to lift her head and/or drop the food or object. At this point, you can begin to kneel down and touch the object before you withdraw, but let your dog keep the object so she perceives your approach as adding to her catch, not taking away from it.

Only when absolutely necessary should you remove your dog's prize or food. When you do, offer her a jack-pot reward.

CONTINUED ON NEXT PAGE

HAND-FEED YOUR DOG

Hand-feeding a dog can be an effective way to bond and overcome dominance issues, including spatial aggression. For guarding and protective breeds, hand-feeding at a young age can help develop devotion and focus.

At your dog's regularly scheduled feeding time, place 50 percent to 100 percent of a meal's kibble in a treat cup or snack pack and direct your dog with basic commands. Here are a few different ways you can try to hand-feed your dog.

Three Methods

METHOD 1: HAND-FEEDING WITH SIT

1. Take one kibble at a time and hold it above your dog's eyes.
2. Bring the kibble back above his ears as you instruct SIT.
3. Guide her into position if necessary using pressure points discussed on page 79.
4. Repeat this sequence five times in a row.

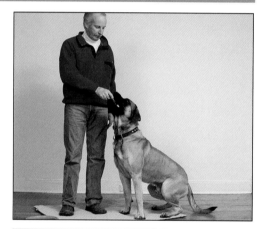

METHOD 2: HAND-FEEDING WITH DOWN

1. From a sit position bring a kibble from your dog's nose to the floor between her paws.
2. Move the treat slowly if your dog is uncooperative.
3. Use the pressure points discussed on page 93 to guide her into position if she needs help.
4. Reward her with praise and a kibble.
5. Repeat this sequence five times in a row before moving onto a different exercise.

METHOD 3: HAND-FEEDING WITH COME

1. Shake your Treat Cup as you call your dog's name and run a few steps away from her.
2. Turn and face your dog and say COME as you pop a kibble in her mouth.
3. Start at varying distances from your dog, gradually extending into another room or by hiding behind the couch or outside behind a bush, tree or building.

Just as you might be agitated when awakened from a deep sleep or a delightful nap, your dog may be equally aggravated. Although it is best to follow the adage "Let sleeping dogs lie," do the following exercises to ensure that your dog does not react unfavorably when waked suddenly. Wake your dog from sleep only once a day.

Approach a Sleeping Pup

1 Approach your dog when she's just fallen into a light snooze. Shake your treat cup as you call her name. The instant she lifts her head, stop, give her a treat, and then walk away.

Progress to waking her from different levels of rest.

2 If you find that your dog startles easily, determine her Red Zone—the closest you can get to her before she gets uncomfortable. Shake your cup, clap, and/or call her name calmly from this distance.

3 If your dog looks confused, kneel down and soothe her with your loving touch and words.

Practice these techniques with your dog in various locations, such as indoors, in the crate, on the furniture, or outside.

Being Around Children

They're impulsive. They're loud. They're a whirl of constant motion. They're kids, and although you may not live with them, your dog is likely to encounter a few in her lifetime, so it is best to condition your dog to accept their differences.

Teach Your Dog to Enjoy Children

MAKE FACE-TO-FACE ENCOUNTERS OKAY

Because of their size, kids are more capable of face-to-face encounters with dogs. Kids also love to stare—it's a sign of normal development. If your dog isn't used to such direct attention, it can be overwhelming. To condition your dog, hold her face in your hands often and stare at her. If your dog is uncomfortable and resistant, place butter or another creamy spread on your hands or arm as you interact in this way.

Kids are also impulsive and are known to climb, trip, and run a lot. This behavior can cause a predatory reaction, and a dog might run, pounce, or mount the child. Start to mimic a child's behavior before introducing your dog so that these activities will seem more commonplace.

When introducing your dog to children, take along treats and butter or another creamy spread. If your dog is familiar with a clicker, this tool can work in your favor, too. Using treats will help your dog form positive associations with being around children. Provided your dog is not showing any signs of aggression, let the kids be involved with handing out the treats and giving direction. If, however, you notice aggressive displays, stop all interactions and call a professional immediately. Don't let your dog become another "dog bites child" statistic.

STEM COMPETITION FOR TOYS

Kids, especially those under age twelve, don't understand object owner-ship and often march right up and take food or toys away from an other-wise content dog. Further, what one has, the other wants. It makes for a lot of screaming and chasing. If you can teach your dog to share (see the earlier section "Teach Your Dog to Share"), it will lower your stress level immeasurably.

ACCLIMATE YOUR DOG TO IMPULSIVITY

They run. They jump. They squeal. All this normal kid impulsiveness can bring out the hunter in even the calmest of dogs. To help your dog learn that children are not prey, practice these exercises:

1. When your dog is relaxed, secure her to a station lead as described on page 39.

2. Tell her to STAY, and then race by. Do not look at her while you go, and don't interact. Repeat STAY if necessary.

3. Wait to praise her until she watches you calmly.

Ask your kids to help, or borrow some chil-dren for this setup:

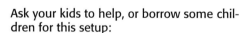

1. With your dog on a leash, stand to the side as the children dart back and forth in front of you.

2. If your dog lurches to chase, tug her back as described on page 110 and remind her to STAY.

CONTINUED ON NEXT PAGE

Teach to Adapt to Children's Voices and Touches

Children have a unique pitch to their voices and a more varied array of intonations. Their touch is also different, used to explore and interact with their environment, not to soothe.

VOICES

Sweet, loud, and sometimes scary, a child often uses her voice to get a reaction from those in her environment, be it a dog or a person, it doesn't seem to matter. Dogs, however, when being "attacked" by a child's inner monster, may interpret this behavior as less than funny. To ensure that your dog is prepared for everything, use different voices and approaches to ready your dog for whatever a child might do.

TOUCH

With children, a bear hug stranglehold is not out of the question. To condition your dog to their often unpredictable expressions of love and sometimes anger, practice hugging, squeezing, prodding, and poking her, treating her and praising her all the while.

TIP

The purpose of handling your dog in preparation for interacting with children is to get her to accept their unpredictability as normal. When the final introductions to the real kids are made, have plenty of treats, toys, and spreadable goodies on hand to further this pleasurable association.

Other Considerations

As you're conditioning your dog to feel more comfortable with children, do not overwhelm her. Do the setups on the previous pages a little at a time. If she is showing signs of stress, such as licking her lips, ducking behind you, nipping, darting at or barking at the children, be more intense with your dramatizations, and ask the children who are helping you to be calmer when they're interacting.

You want your dog to see children as an invitation to play and relax and to get extra rewards and loving. To emphasize this, remember the following:

- Let your dog drag a leash when children are around. This will give you a calm way to interfere if she gets overstimulated or frightened.

- Have treats and toys on hand whenever your dog is around children. If you are using a clicker, this is the time to take it out. Praise and interact with your dog more often.

- Teach the children how to communicate with your dog. Simple directions like SIT, games found in chapter 9, and fun tricks—all rewarded with praise, treats, and/or toys—are ways to ensure that everyone has fun.

- If your dog is truly overexcited or withdrawn, use a Gentle Leader to help calm her. (See page 188.)

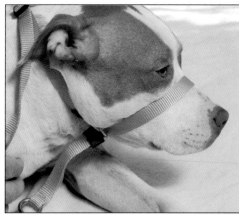

Adapting to Environmental Sounds

Many sights and sounds are so commonplace that we humans don't even notice them. But dogs, especially puppies, are often overwhelmed by these nuisances. How you react when your dog responds to her environment will make the difference between a dog who acts appropriately and one who falls apart or becomes aggressive.

When working to help your dog overcome her fears, look at things from her perspective. Your dog hears much better than you do, and her nose is considerably more reliable. She depends on these senses to interpret her surroundings. She relies on her vision only to decipher movement and posturing. Can you imagine what a helmeted human wielding a jackhammer must seem like?

OUTDOOR MAINTENANCE

The fact that lawn mowers, hedge trimmers, and similar machines are often operated around your dog's home environment is a clear indication of why they are so disliked by your dog. "Big, loud beasts" is what they may seem like to your dog. Start handling her at a distance from the offending machine, giving her commands and rewarding her cooperation.

With your dog on leash, move progressively closer to the work that is setting her off. If she becomes aggressive, call for professional help. No one likes to be bitten. Keep your dog at your side and behind you to communicate your role as her guardian and protector.

THUNDER

Many dogs harbor a distinct fear of thunder. Whether the fear stems from changes in barometric pressure or the sheer intensity of the noise is often debated, but there's no mistaking a dog's reaction to it. Panting, pacing, tub-sitting, or tearing at enclosures are all signs of anxiety of differing intensities.

When helping your dog overcome her fear of thunder, stay calm, cool, and collected. Keep her on a leash, or a head collar to avoid choking, and act like it's a sunny day. Be the example of serenity; your dog will be impressed.

CONSTRUCTION

The loud, erratic sounds and strange machinery found on construction sites combine to create a scene that can put the hair up on any dog's back. First, handle your dog at a distance she's comfortable with, treating her for responding to your direction. As she gains confidence, move toward these sites. Continue to direct and reward her. If your dog becomes suddenly timid, move away from the site, and then work your way back.

SIRENS

Many dogs are startled by the sound of a siren. In fact, the myriad sounds of a city can make it a confusing environment and an impossible place for your dog to relax. Consider your dog's hearing when a siren passes close by: cover her ears with your hands. Introduce your dog to urban sounds in a controlled fashion. Train or play with her near a fire station at noon, for example: you'll both hear the noon whistle blow!

Although it's tempting to soothe a dog at the sound of a siren, that reaction often has the reverse effect—your soft tones and bent posture convey fear, not reassurance, to your dog.

TRAIN WHISTLES

The same rules apply here as with sirens. If you live near a train track, you'll also want to train your dog to run from the train (and not chase it) when she sees one coming. For tips on how to approach that task, flip to page 185 and follow the instructions for car chasing.

If train stations are to be a part of your life, it will be helpful to do several training sessions there to ensure your dog's focus and her confidence in your direction regardless of the distractions.

FIREWORKS

Although fireworks are likely to light up the night sky only once a year, that single day claims the sanity of many dogs, who run off or claw the house in utter terror. Start by introducing light fireworks in the daylight, mingling with your dog at a distance at which she feels comfortable, and using treats to develop a positive association. Gradually increase your dog's accessibility to fireworks. Do not, however, shoot them at your dog. As she gets more confident, you can try an evening display.

Note: *When moving closer to a distraction, use the direction HEEL and keep your dog behind you. Your forward position communicates that you—and not she—will be the protector.*

FAQ

Why does my dog seem to get even more nervous when I tell her, "It's okay?"

Your dog interprets the high pitch of your voice as a whine, your focus as a sign of confusion, and your body posture as submissive. Stand tall, be positive and relaxed, and your confidence will surely rub off on her.

Coping with Household Noises

There is a specific period in a young puppy's development when everyday household distractions are integrated normally. This is known as the socialization period, and it falls between eight and fourteen weeks of age. If your dog did not have this experience as a pup, she may have exaggerated responses to objects you use daily.

Common Noises

VACUUMS AND OTHER APPLIANCES

Many dogs are either cautious or hyper with vacuums. The noise factor and the shape of the object are difficult for them to translate. The worst thing you can do is to chase or tease your dog with the vacuum. Whether it is the vacuum, the coffee maker, or some other appliance that leaves your dog perplexed and frightened, introduce it to her this way:

1 Let her see the object unplugged. Place it in the middle of the floor and lace its border with yummy treats.

2 Manipulate the object without turning it on. Do not look at or interact with your dog as you do so.

3 Ask a helper to turn on the object in the next room as you practice lessons or play games with your dog.

4 Gradually move closer to the object until you can work the appliance yourself without your dog overreacting to it.

POTS AND PANS

The sound of metal against metal or flooring can send dogs into a jag of barking from which it is hard to recover. In this case, work or play with your dog at decreasing distances, using rewards and praise until she is more comfortable with the sound.

DOORBELL

The sound of a doorbell is very exciting for a dog: change, visitors, and the potential for attention do a lot to spark a dog's interest. And wild behavior is generally reinforced immediately: although you wouldn't let me knock you out of the way to greet your company, you might be more permissive with your dog. Shouts and pushes signal clear disapproval to any human, but to a dog they're perceived as hyper, physical play.

The first step in teaching appropriate greeting manners is to reclaim your door. Practice the waiting skill taught on page 80, and enforce containment each time you leave or reenter your home. Also, create a station near the door to allow your dog to interact but not interfere.

SHOUTING

Although a shouting match can be a cathartic experience for humans, it can frighten a dog. To help your dog cope, designate a safe area, such as a crate or a corner, to send her to, and take heated discussions out of the room.

5

Puppy Kindergarten: Early Conditioning

The neat thing about puppies is that they haven't experienced anything yet. Their minds are free from worries. They think they are perfect just the way they are, and if you approach training with the same outlook—that your puppy is perfect just the way he is—you both will have a much more pleasant experience.

That said, puppies can be really frustrating. They have a lot of energy. Their curiosity is constant, and they explore everything—with their mouths. In fact, it would be unusual if a puppy didn't make house-training mistakes, chew, nip, run wild circles around the floor, and jump to say hello. These misbehaviors, as you might call them, are all actually wonderful signs of a puppy who is developing and bonding normally.

The goal of this chapter, aimed at puppies who are two to six months old, is to help you understand your puppy's motivations, impulses, and needs in order to better prepare you for the months ahead. Knowing what to expect, and knowing that your frustrations are shared and are normal, will help you separate your feelings from the daily realities that may overwhelm you sometimes. In addition, you can use the many exercises in this chapter to condition your young pup to commands and routines that will shape your lives together.

Meeting Your Puppy's Needs

Puppies under twelve weeks are a lot like human babies. Their daily existence is motivated by five basic needs: to eat, drink, sleep, go to the bathroom, and play. The degree to which they bond with you is directly determined by your capacity to meet each need and provide an environment as stress free as possible.

Yelling at or trying to discipline a puppy is as silly as yelling at a baby for knocking over a glass. All you create is a sense of fear and confusion. In fact, the bond you are trying to form—a bond of trust and direction—will be broken because the very person your puppy needs to turn to when he is frightened is the one frightening him.

Although there are many similarities between puppies and children, including their instinct to communicate their needs as they arise, there is a significant difference. When a baby has a need, he or she cries. It is then the parent's responsibility to interpret that cry and take care of the need. The parent doing so forms trust. Puppies, on the other hand, don't cry—they nip and get fidgety. If your puppy needs to poop or is tired, for example, that feeling will confuse him, and in reaction to that confusion, he will nip whomever he is attached to: namely you. Interestingly, this is a good sign: if your puppy is nipping you, it shows that he loves you and wants your help in figuring out his system. Instead of reacting to the nipping with frustration, think about which of his needs might be pressing. Try to meet that need by taking him out or putting him in his crate or quiet area to nap.

As babies grow, they are taught words so that they can communicate each need: "I have to go potty," "I'm hungry," even just "water." These words are all primitive, yet recognizable, ways a developing child can get her needs met without crying. Although your dog can't talk, you can teach him the meaning of short words or phrases to correspond to specific routines. Within a month, your puppy will simply go to the door and ring a bell to go outside, or stand by the water bowl or put himself to rest, instead of nipping you.

An easy way to organize and address your puppy's needs is to create a needs chart. You will use three columns: the first specifies each need, the second identifies a specific word, and the third gives you a routine to follow consistently so that your puppy will know how to signal his needs as they arise. Show your chart to everyone in your household—consistency and repetition create understanding and cooperation.

Needs Chart		
Need	*Word*	*Routine*
Eat	HUNGRY	Schedule feeding times. Place the bowl in the same spot and encourage SIT before feeding.
Drink	WATER	Keep the bowl in the same spot. Encourage SIT.
Bathroom	OUTSIDE/PAPERS and GET BUSY	Follow the same route to the same spot. Use a bell to encourage a signal. Restrict attention until he goes.
Rest	ON YOUR MAT or TIME FOR BED	Designate one spot in each shared room. Take puppy to a mat/bed, provide a chew, and secure him if necessary.
Play	BONE, BALL, or TOY and GO PLAY!	Establish a play area inside and out. Make sure that all four paws are on the floor before you toss a toy or give a treat.

Say YES More Than NO and Say It Often

You'll need to exercise a lot of self-control when your puppy is active, defiant, or testing you. If you get angry, you may accidentally encourage mischief, as your puppy will do anything to get your attention, regardless of whether it's negative or positive.

Your goal is to highlight the times your puppy is doing the right things and cooperating rather than wait to interfere when he's naughty. Simple logic tells you that he'll repeat the behaviors you reward because they satisfy his need for attention and his craving to fulfill his needs.

If you're sharing your puppy with family and friends, it's important that they follow the same logic. One happy solution is to select one word—for example, YES or GOOD—to highlight all the moments your puppy is cooperating. One strong happy bark–sounding word is actually better than a string of "good puppy, good puppy, good puppy," which may by mistake end on a bad behavior.

Use your encouragement word for everything your puppy is doing right, which is to say everything he is not doing wrong! When you focus on good behavior, from licking, to chewing on a bone, to interacting calmly with the kids, you'll be surprised by what your puppy comes up with! Pair this word with an upbeat hand signal, and your puppy will not only be listening to you he'll be looking for your direction as well!

Structure Spaces

A chaotic, cluttered household will really confuse your puppy. He's so new, everything warrants a thorough investigation. Not an issue when the floor's clear, but when it's cluttered it's hard for a puppy to mind his manners. Consider a neat environment versus a messy one: which makes you feel more settled?

When organizing your home, think of everything from your puppy's perspective. Put yourself in his paws, getting right down to his level. Remember, everything looks different when you're looking up from the floor.

Your Puppy's Spaces

FOOD AND WATER

Designate a place for your puppy's food and water dishes. Each time you feed him or give him water, put the bowl down in this spot. Place all dishes out of heavily trafficked areas.

If you have a large home or yard, place multiple water dishes so that they are accessible.

POTTY AREA

Whether you are training your puppy to go outside or on papers, select a specific area for him to potty, and be consistent. Consider toilet training a child: you don't place potties in the middle of the floor or send your child to the neighbor's house to use the bathroom.

QUIET PLACES FOR REST AND SLEEP

As you introduce your puppy to different areas of the house, consider where you want him to go. Just as you would direct a person to sit in a chair, you need to direct your puppy to a bed or mat on which to rest, and help him organize his toys there. Remember that puppies are very social, and your puppy will be happiest being near you. Use a specific direction like SETTLE DOWN when leading him to his area.

Select areas to send your puppy when you're eating, watching TV, reading, or working. See "Displacement Activities" on page 73, and provide your puppy with some favorite objects to keep him occupied while you're busy.

Be mindful of a restless puppy. Restlessness indicates that other needs, perhaps exercise or play, are pressing. It is your responsibility as his "parent" to take care of his needs.

FREE PLAY AREA

Having your puppy bound wildly around your home can be very disruptive. He will also have to go to the bathroom during and following a play bout, which is reason enough to put some parameters on his freedom. Create play areas and decide on games the whole family can play to give him a sense of structure as well as a sense of fun!

TIP

You must decide if you want your adult dog on the furniture. If you don't want a dog who shares the furniture with you, don't confuse your puppy by inviting him onto the couch. Give your puppy a specific place to lie—such as at one end of the furniture or on the floor—and be consistent with that direction.

Condition Your Puppy to Wear a Collar and Leash

Getting your puppy comfortable with a collar and a leash can be like getting a child to accept lace or wool for the first time. Some acclimate without complaint, others who are more sensitive protest wildly. Your reactions should be non-eventful. Place each on for twenty-minute increments, following the below instructions until your puppy fully accepts each.

Collars and Leashes

COLLAR

The first time you put a collar on your puppy, he may not like it. He may stop, sit, and scratch or twist in the air in an attempt to free himself of the encumbrance. Don't worry. Leave the collar on for twenty-minute periods throughout the day. Soon it will feel like part of his skin.

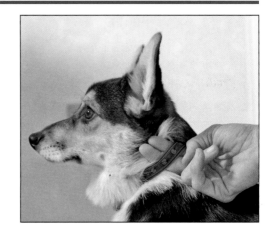

Your puppy is going to grow fast, so check his collar frequently to prevent tightness. Make sure you're able to slip two fingers comfortably between his neck and collar. If you select a harness for your puppy, the same rules apply. Harnesses can be harder to fit, so take your puppy to the pet store, and ask a professional for assistance in finding one suited for your particular puppy.

LEASH

Your puppy's first leash should be light-weight and flexible. Let him drag it initially until he's used to the weight behind him. Don't worry if he picks up the leash and chews it; this is normal behavior. If he's destroying the leash, provide a suitable alternative for him to chew, and spray the leash with Bitter Apple. Once your puppy is comfortable with its weight, condition him to walk with you.

1. Pick up the lead and follow him.

2. When he looks back at you, praise him, YES, and/or offer him a treat or toy. Continue to use rewards to encourage his focus when you hold the leash.

③ Gradually put pressure on the leash as you follow him.

④ Using a treat cup (see page 42) and enthusiastic movements and praise, begin to step away and encourage him to follow you. Use consistent words to teach your puppy to follow your lead, such as LET'S GO!

Note: Remember the voice rule. Your puppy will want to follow your voice when it is moving away from him. Don't yell at your puppy to follow you.

Once your puppy is confident on the leash inside, try it in increasingly more distracting environments, such as outside or with family or visitors. Follow the same cycle as above—initially walk your puppy on a loose lead, highlighting each time he looks to you, using food or toy rewards; progress slowly to greater pressure. As you encourage your puppy to follow you, use rewards and toys to sustain his interest in your direction.

Encourage him to follow you by throwing your voice in the opposite direction. Act like you've found a really neat treasure that you want to share. Reward his cooperation.

Ultimately, insist that your puppy follow you. Use food and toys to lead him initially.

Introduce Stairs

Many puppies are thrown off by stairs: their eyes can't make sense of the depth and angle. Although it is tempting to soothe and carry your puppy, resist this habit. It will only teach him to be helpless. Instead, encourage a can-do mentality.

Stairs

1. With a helper and some treats, approach the stairs with your puppy in your arms. Carry him to the third step from the top or bottom. Place him down gently.

2. Without talking, support your puppy's rib cage to alleviate his fear of falling.

3. Have your helper stand at the top or bottom of the stairs and excite your puppy with food or toys. If your puppy is frozen with fear, use your hands to guide him through the motion of walking the steps.

4. Repeat this process again and again, gradually increasing the number of steps your puppy must tackle. Look at him, talk to him, and praise him when he accomplishes this task, not when he avoids it!

Believe it or not, you can teach your puppy the human equivalent of saying please. It's not a vocal equivalent, but a very civilized behavior nonetheless. He will learn to sit whenever he wants something, from asking to be let out to requesting food or attention. Before offering your puppy anything he considers positive, direct him to SIT. Position him immediately if he is too excited or distracted to mind you.

Leave a leash on your puppy if he's a wild jumper. Step on the leash so that he has only enough room to get a few inches off the ground before feeling tugged. If the jumping occurs at mealtimes, put his food and water dishes down only after he is calm and is sitting.

Do not let your puppy jump up and grab toys out of your hand. If you're holding a toy and your puppy jumps at you, lift the toy above your head. Reintroduce the toy and release or toss it only after your puppy is sitting.

Repeat the same sequence with treats. Offer your puppy a treat by holding it above his head. If he jumps, lift it up. Reintroduce it, offering the snack only after your dog is sitting calmly.

When your dog approaches you for a pat or a belly rub, ask him to SIT first. Pawing, staring, or whining is an uncivilized way to get attention. When your dog sits, it is the canine equivalent of saying please.

A puppy under six months of age cannot understand the concept of NO. As a puppy, he lacks the impulse control to forget about whatever is distracting him.

Avoid using NO when addressing your puppy. You will end up saying it too frequently and it will lose both its message and its power. A simple EP, EP gently discourages your puppy. When he can understand right from wrong (five to six months of age), you can begin to use the direction NO.

EP, EP

When you catch your puppy's curiosity leading him astray, say EP, EP in a gently discouraging tone. For example, if you see him heading toward a tissue basket or starting to jump on the couch, interfere by saying EP, EP. The words are best reinforced with a short directional tug of the collar. Avoid touching your puppy when you do so, as any touch is perceived as interactive. If grasping your puppy's collar is difficult, attach a short drag lead (see page 35) for easier intervention.

FAQ

My puppy knows what NO means—he cowers every time I shout at him—but at the same time, he's not too bright. He goes right back to the behavior, and I have to yell at him again. Help!

Your puppy is not dumb. He's repeating the behavior because he knows it will result in interaction—negative or positive just doesn't matter. And although he may look like he understands you, what you are seeing is pure fear. Fear is a completely ineffective training tool.

Flip to pages 84–85 for a more thorough explanation of teaching NO.

To ensure cooperation, when you visit the vet, go into town and resting while you eat, provide your dog with a displacement activity, such as a bone or a toy. It is like providing a young child with a coloring book or a video game.

Displacement Activities

If your hope is that your puppy will stay with you while you relax with a good book, give him a comfortable place to sit and a good bone to chew. Have one special chew bone or object that your puppy only sees at dinnertime or when company visits. Stuffing a little peanut butter into his regular chew can be exciting. Use this object for those times when you really need your dog to calm down.

If suddenly your puppy starts to fidget, ask yourself if he needs to go out or wants some water. Pet him when he's calm.

Take your displacement activities on the road, too. They'll help your puppy relax at his doctor's or while you're at the café.

TIP

For every behavior that frustrates you, think of something you'd like your dog to be doing instead—that is a displacement activity. Your puppy can displace his need for oral interaction by licking instead of nipping. He can displace his instinct for chasing a cat, by running after a ball or swing toy. He can displace his impulse to jump on visitors by racing around with a toy or ball.

Puppy Point

The puppy point is a magical hand signal that teaches your puppy to look, as well as listen, to you for direction.

Give Direction by Pointing

1. Extend your index finger in a pronounced point.
2. Hold your index finger out one inch from your puppy's nose.
3. When he touches your finger with his nose, mark the moment with praise, or a click, and a reward.
4. Repeat this process ten times.

5. Take a step backward and point between your legs.
6. React happily when he races over.

7 Play with your new skill:

Move your point above his head and guide him into a sitting position.

Point between his front paws and guide him into a down position.

When you want him near you, call his name and point to the exact spot you want him to be.

6

Grade-School Lessons

As your puppy ages or your dog ventures past adolescence, you'll notice some changes in her behavior—many of them not fun or pretty. She may take matters into her own hands and disregard any direction from you. In fact, there may be times when she looks at you as though you've never met before. Don't be offended. These are signs of a naturally maturing or as-yet-untrained dog. Things don't have to go on like this forever. Although you may feel as though your dog is stupid, these displays of independence are often signs of high intelligence that has been misdirected. Don't despair—the solution to your frustration is just ahead.

The best way to introduce and enforce the basic commands introduced in this chapter is to integrate them into your daily routine with your dog. Highlight a word a week, and share the plan with your family and friends. Ask everyone to use the word before your dog receives anything positive. For example, everyone can use the word SIT before giving treats, food, water, petting, or freedom.

The Magic Five

As you establish your position as leader and train your dog how to behave in all situations, teach her the Magic Five: foundation commands that will form the basis for your life together.

LET'S GO

This direction says follow me. It is not an option, but you don't have to be harsh about driving that point home.

1. Secure your dog's leash to your waist, or hold half the leash in your relaxed arms.

2. Walk forward, saying LET'S GO.

3. If your dog races ahead, calmly turn away from her—to the right if she is on your left side—and repeat NAME, LET'S GO. Turn as often as necessary until your dog realizes that she'd better watch you for direction. When she does, reward her enthusiastically with food and praise.

SIT

Give this nonoptional direction only when you're able to follow through by positioning your dog. If she doesn't listen, don't repeat yourself; simply position her immediately, as shown.

1 Place your right hand under your dog's chin or her collar. Lift up gently as you coordinate this motion with the next step.

2 Brace her by placing your thumb and index finger on your dog's waist muscle and squeeze gently as you lift under her chin.

3 Repeat SIT as your dog relaxes into this position.

CONTINUED ON NEXT PAGE

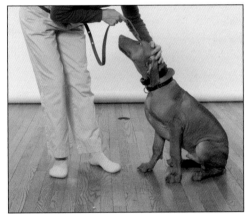

TIP

Avoid pressing on your dog's backbone. Aside from being discomforting, it will cause her to resist and challenge your direction. Instead, squeeze the waist muscle, which is located just behind your dog's ribcage.

WAIT and OKAY

These two directions, when used together, tell your dog to look to you for permission and assurance before crossing thresholds and streets.

1 Place your dog on a leash and position her at your side. Hold her back, repeating WAIT until she relaxes. (If this process takes more time than you have, consider buying a training collar.)

2 When she does relax, say OKAY and proceed.

TIP

The direction to WAIT is about impulse control and focus. When practicing this command, try it in various situations, from food control to stairs, doors, and curbs.

EXCUSE ME

Teach your dog to respect your space: use a polite but crisply stated EXCUSE ME anytime she blocks your path or leans against you. If you wouldn't let a family member crowd you, don't let your dog. If she resists moving gently move her aside with your knee or foot.

Note: *The directions LET'S GO and EXCUSE ME passively communicate your team captain status. Each command demands recognition and respect, but do it in a subtle, nonconfrontational manner.*

SETTLE and BONE

Use these two directions together to teach your dog to go to her play station on cue.

1 As you lead your dog to the play station, point and say SETTLE.

2 When you get there, say BONE and offer her something to chew.

Leading

Teach your dog to walk on a leash (or *lead*) throughout your home, holding her leash loosely in your left hand or securing it around your waist. Think of the leash as giving you the capacity to hold your dog's hand and guide her. These same techniques work beautifully outdoors.

Lead Your Dog

1 Secure the leash around your waist like a belt or hold it in your left hand with your arms relaxed at your sides.

2 Bring your dog to your left side.

3 Walk forward calmly, calling out your dog's name and LET'S GO.

4 If your dog races ahead, turn away from her (to the right) and walk in the opposite direction. Repeat as often as necessary to catch your dog's attention. Look at her and praise her when she's walking next to you on a loose leash.

5 Walk throughout your home, practicing the foundation commands listed on the previous pages.

FAQ

Why do trainers always recommend walking dogs on the left side?

As most people are right-handed, convenience demands that dogs walk on the opposite side so as not to interfere.

My dog is unmanageable in certain areas of my home. What should I do?

Do not let her into those areas unsupervised. Take her into the rooms by leading her, showing her how to contain her impulses.

Most people teach NO as an interactive direction—shouting NO while a dog is in the middle of misbehaving. Instead of teaching anything constructive, it is often perceived as interactive play or, worse, as an overwhelming threat. Neither perception provides any long-term learning value. When a dog is in the middle of destroying, stealing, chasing, or going potty, the thought to do these things has already passed: your reaction is seen as interactive, not instructional. NO in these instances sets up a vicious cycle that often increases misbehavior.

Teach NO

To teach your dog the meaning of the word NO, you need to catch her in the thought process; to do so, you must organize lessons until your dog understands them. If you interfere with the action itself, your dog will think you're participating, and the behavior may get more frequent or intense.

Before you set up situations (see pages 84–85) to teach your dog the meaning of NO, decide what a good displacement activity will be. For example, if you don't want her to nip you, KISSES might be a better alternative. If you don't want your dog to chew a slipper, have a suitable toy on hand to replace it. Design a table of behaviors and substitutes, and share it with all parties involved in your dog's training.

Behavior	Response with NO	Displacement Activity
Chewing	Pull back on the leash; correct the object	Direct to area SETTLE and BONE
Nipping	Pull away	KISSES or to specific need
Going potty in an inappropriate place	Clap/interrupt thought	OUTSIDE/PAPERS
Jumping	Use leash to head off	GET TOY or SIT or BELLY UP
Chasing	Leash correction	TOY or other focusing commands (SIT, DOWN)

Discourage Chewing with NO

Make a list of your dog's favorite things to chew or steal. Now, make a list of suitable alternatives—bones or toys that she adores playing with. If she has none, find at least three things immediately.

Teach the Concept of NO

To encourage chewing on appropriate things, start playing with her toys throughout the day. Steal a toy, shake it in front of her face, and run away and hide.

Set up the following situation to teach your dog to avoid her unsuitable favorites (your things).

1. Place an object, such as a paper towel or a shoe, in the middle of the floor.

2. Walk your dog into the room on a leash.

3. The moment she shows interest in the object, pull back on the leash and say NO.

4. Shout at the object. That's right—at the object, not at your dog. Don't even look at your dog—you are communicating that the object is bad and that your dog should avoid it.

5. Walk your dog by the object until she avoids even looking at it.

6. Redirect your dog to her BONE or TOY. Good job!

You can apply the same techniques to other household objects, such as wastepaper baskets and dishwashers. The same rule applies: set up the situation and correct the thought process. Once your dog is in the midst of misbehaving, you're too late to make an impression—if that's the case, calmly separate her and let it go.

Once your dog begins to understand that NO means to curb her impulse, you can use it in other situations, such as keeping her from chasing a cat or a child: no correcting the object required!

If your dog is a cat-chasing addict, take the two animals into a small bathroom with your dog on a leash and training collar. The moment she looks to your cat, pull back on the leash and say NO and give another direction, like SIT or DOWN. Continue this process until the two of them can sit comfortably together in a small room. Gradually enlarge the space until your dog is able to contain her impulses indoors and out.

Set up other situations in a similar way. If she can't keep her tongue off the plates in the dishwasher, bring her into the kitchen on her leash and training collar. Open the dishwasher, and the moment she's temped to check it out, pull back and say NO. Without further hesitation, correct the dishes. Bang a wooden spoon to a pot: BAD DISH. Ignore your dog as you do this and redirect him to a bone and bed when your point has been made.

If you catch your dog about to have an accident, interfere with a NO and hurry her to her potty area.

Point Training

Point training is a valuable lesson in communicating with your dog. I introduced a playful point in chapter 5, but if you're starting with an older dog, you can teach this skill at any time. It will train your dog to look to you and follow the point of your finger for all directions, from SIT to greeting company civilly to performing tricks.

Follow the Point

There are three steps to point training: the initial point (see above), moving the lure, and directing with the lure. All of them involve helping your dog follow the point of your finger. Ensure that your signal is crisp by using your index finger.

Teach point training as a game, using treats and toys in the initial stages. Although you will fade off lures in a couple of weeks, continue to praise your dog.

INSTANT REWARD

Sandwich a goody between your middle finger and your thumb. Prepare your point signal with the same hand. Initially point no more than a few inches from your dog. When she reaches out to your finger, mark the moment (say YES or click) and reward her with what you're holding. Continue to practice this, pointing within close range until you see that your dog is catching on. Gradually increase the distance she must move to your finger as well as the number of successful touches she must make to get the treat.

DELAYED RESPONSE

Place some goodies in a snack pack or pocket. Point at close range. When your dog goes to your finger, mark the moment and reward her by pulling a treat from the secondary location. Increase the distance slowly, no longer rewarding her the instant she cooperates, but making sure to mark the second she reaches the point, and then treat a few seconds later. Slowly increase the delay between the point and the treat.

Gradually phase off treating your dog for every successful point, but always mark the moment with an enthusiastic YES! Good dog!

In real life, use the point to signal your dog to move in a certain direction or into a certain position. The point will also help her feel calmer with unfamiliar settings or people.

TIP

As you extend the pause between a successful point and the treat you'll notice your dog's focus sharpening. Look to your dog when she watches you and praise her increasing attention span.

HEEL

This direction tells your dog to follow along at your heel. If you could converse with her in English, you'd be saying, "I'm the leader—follow me." Since leaders lead, you will need to teach your dog to walk behind you.

Teach Your Dog HEEL

Three ingredients will simplify your lessons:

- Relax with the idea. You are simply teaching your dog to walk behind you.

- Find a suitable, effective training collar (see page 32). The collar can make or break a dog's understanding. It needs to convey comfort and praise when the dog is near you and discomfort and disapproval when she surges ahead.

- Choose the right leash. Make sure that the leash you select is made of a comfortable material, is the right weight for your dog, and is between four and six feet long. Retractable leashes are not appropriate for training.

Teach the command HEEL in an undistracting environment, such as a living room or a backyard. Practice twice a day for ten minutes. Continue this routine for five days or until your dog is familiar and cooperative with this direction.

DIRECTED HEEL

1 Walk your dog in a large counterclockwise circle to start.

2 Bring your dog to your left side, using treats to lure her.

3 Sit her down next to your left heel, positioning her if necessary.

4 Say NAME, HEEL as you walk forward. Maintain a balanced rhythm as you walk, using a quick tug on the leash to position your dog at your heel if she pulls.

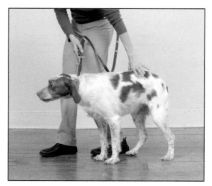

5 As you complete your circle, grasp the leash with your right hand and use your left hand to position your dog into a sitting posture. You are teaching her to stop and sit when you stop. HEEL is a command of position as well as of walking control.

Your dog may start out rambunctious. This is normal, especially if leash walks have been chaotic in the past. Stay calm and repeat your circles again and again. Time and repetition are good teaching tools.

CONTINUED ON NEXT PAGE

OVERCOME OBJECTIONS

If your dog is overpowering you, slide the leash behind your back and hold it with two straight arms. When she pulls forward, push back on the leash with your bottom. Use the trunk of your body to manage and control her.

If your dog stops in her tracks, determine whether she is afraid or offering passive resistance. If it's passive resistance, continue walking. If she's truly overwhelmed, go back to a familiar room, review the leash-training techniques outlined earlier in this chapter, and/or use food or toys to lure her forward. Avoid retracing your steps, as this will reinforce her behavior. Lure her forward to you.

When you stop, your dog may try to shuffle about. Don't let her. There's only one way to sit or stand at a heel, and it is right next to you. Use the pressure points discussed on page 93 and a gentle reminder to HEEL as you position her.

INCREASE DISTRACTIONS

Gradually increase distractions to meet your dog's increasing attention span. For example, have a member of your family nearby, eating or playing games. Ask them not to interrupt the lesson, however. Give your dog a confident HEEL and begin to walk in straight lines—you may notice that your dog is suddenly more distractible. Don't stop or look at her, as these changes in pace indicate insecurity on your part. Walk with a self-assured posture and maintain the same rhythm. If your dog hesitates or lunges, give her a quick tug back to your heel. Praise all cooperation.

Introduce HEEL on your walks. Anytime you are off your property, one of you must lead and the other must follow. If you've been the follower, it's time to switch roles. A dog who leads does not train well or mind reliably. Use HEEL to communicate the change in status.

CONTINUED ON NEXT PAGE

 TIP

What if my dog has to go potty during her walk?
Your dog should be going potty close to your home, which will help you avoid assertive encounters with other people and dogs along the walk. If she must go, take her to a specified area and release her to go potty. Once through (give her no more than three minutes), call her back to HEEL and finish your walk. Let her go potty near your home once more before you go inside.

HANDS-FREE HEELING

If you're feeling relaxed with your dog, you can start to direct her hands-free. Either attach or tie the leash around your waist or lay it over your shoulder.

1 Go back and practice small circles.

2 If your dog moves out of place, quickly grasp the leash (as though it were a hot wire) and tug back to your side.

3 Gradually increase the distractions as suggested above.

TIP

If your dog is working well in low-distraction environments but can't stay focused when others are around, do not push her. Think of the leash as holding her hand, and gently guide her when she can't concentrate.

DOWN is one of the most important directions that you will teach your dog. That said, it can be challenging to learn and may take time to perfect. Your goal is to have your dog calmly lie down when you point to the floor and/or say DOWN.

After you teach your dog the DOWN, she'll respect your judgment, trust your direction, and calm down on cue. There are three phases to teaching this command: tell and show, straight back, and standing down.

Tell and Show

Introduce the DOWN command in a cheerful manner. Use it throughout the day when feeding your dog or when playing with toys. There are two ways to encourage your dog's cooperation at this stage in training:

- Use treats/toys to lure her into position, saying DOWN as she relaxes into the position. When using a lure, lower the object from her nose to the space between her paws.

- Locate the pressure point between your dog's shoulder blades and apply gentle pressure with a flat thumb to position her. If she still resists, lift a paw gently to create a tripod effect.

CONTINUED ON NEXT PAGE

TIP

Does your dog want nothing to do with this command? You can play-train her by sitting on the floor with a knee bent, and baiting your dog under your leg. When she is forced to lie down to follow the treat, say DOWN and reward her lovingly.

Straight Back

Once your dog is cooperating enthusiastically, you're ready to teach her a more formal response to the direction. Your goal is to be able to point and say DOWN without lowering yourself into the position.

1 Sit in a chair with your back straight, or kneel on the floor, remaining upright.

2 Instruct DOWN by pointing with your right hand. (If you are using treats/toys, keep them on the counter or in a snack pack.)

3 If your dog hesitates, put steady pressure between her shoulders and guide her into position. Pause, praise, release her with an OKAY, and reward her. Vary the duration of the pause before you release her so that she learns to concentrate on your direction rather than preempt you.

Standing DOWN

For the final phase, remember your goal: to be able to calmly direct your dog DOWN regardless of the environment or its distractions. To do so, you must be able to stand upright; if you always bend and point, your dog will need you to do so 100 percent of the time. If you've mastered the straight-back DOWN, you're ready for the final phase—DOWN from a standing position.

1 Put your dog on her leash and take her to a quiet room.

2 Slide the leash under your foot discreetly, stand tall, and say/signal DOWN.

3 As you say it, you may bend at the knees, but not at the back. If your dog needs a hint, slide the leash up to remind her. (Do not use the leash to choke your dog into position. Apply only slight pressure.)

CONTINUED ON NEXT PAGE

TIP

Use hand signals to increase your dog's visual focus:

- DOWN: Point straight down from your dog's nose to the floor between her paws.
- SIT: Sweep upward with a pointed finger from your dog's nose to your eyes.
- STAY: Flash a flat palm in front of your dog's nose and remove it quickly.
- OKAY: Sweep out from your dog's nose with a pointed finger as you step forward.

4 If she still resists, position her gently. Pause and praise. Good dog! Practice three to ten downs per lesson, mixed in with other directions like HEEL and STAY.

5 Once your dog goes down willingly, pivot directly in front of her and follow the same pattern, progressively moving away from her one foot at a time.

TIP

Once your dog is cooperating, use the word DOWN whenever it applies: when you're waiting at the veterinarian's, during quiet times at home with friends and family, and to remind her to calm down when she acts impulsively. If your dog ignores you, position her calmly. Like SIT and COME, DOWN is not a word to be repeated.

COME

The human equivalent to COME is the word *huddle*. It should be taught as an upbeat bonding exercise that reinforces your togetherness, not your separation.

There are three phases to the COME exercise: name association, reconnection, and come from a distance. Practice each phase individually before linking them together.

Teach Name Association

Help your dog make a positive association with her name.

1 Call her name and mark the moment she looks to you with praise or other rewards.

Note: You can also use a clicker or a target word to mark the moment your dog comes to yours your side.

2 Shake a treat cup, calling your dog's name as you run away from her. Throw your voice away from your dog when calling her. Praise her attention.

Note: Use a strong directional tone when calling to your dog, similar to the one a football quarterback would use to give directions in a huddle. Sound confident and enthusiastic.

CONTINUED ON NEXT PAGE

Reconnection

Before calling your dog from a distance, teach her that the direction COME is a command to be together, not apart. It's about connection, interaction, and warmth, not separation and hostility. Eventually, when she hears COME across a field or yard, she will race over to be near you.

When your dog approaches you for attention, say COME and point from her eyes to yours to get her attention. Praise her warmly. You can also approach her with treats in your pocket to reinforce the idea.

When playing with a favorite toy, say COME and bring your dog's attention to your eyes. Toss the toy enthusiastically.

COME from a Distance

When introducing COME from a distance, begin with small separations.

① Step back from a six-foot leash and call your dog: NAME, COME.

② If you're able, step or run backward.

③ Gather the leash as your dog moves toward you.

④ Physically interact with, praise, and reward her when she is close.

CONTINUED ON NEXT PAGE

As you increase the separation, use other leashes, such as a retractable leash or a long line. Try the following exercises to highlight this direction:

- As you call to your dog, throw your voice in the opposite direction.
- Call to your dog as you play with sticks or one of her favorite toys.

- Hide behind a building or a tree and call to your dog. Shake a treat cup if your dog gets confused.
- Play the Runaway Come game (see page 146).

FAQ

These exercises work great on-leash, but off-leash my dog ignores me. What should I do?

Don't expect the same focus from your dog off-leash at this point. We'll concentrate more on that in the next chapter. If you're in a situation where you need to get your dog but she's off-leash, simply use her name and run from her, or get some treats and pretend to eat them by yourself. Do not look at or call to her—wait until she's near and grasp her collar gently.

This direction is good for many things, from grooming and wiping muddy paws to standing still for petting.

Teach Your Dog STAND

1 Kneel down on the floor next to your dog and place your right hand, palm out, on your dog's buckle collar.

2 Slide your left hand under your dog's belly.

3 Say STAND as you gently prop your dog into a standing position.

CONTINUED ON NEXT PAGE

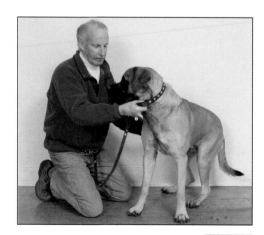

④ Relax your right hand on your dog's collar, and slide your left hand to rest on your dog's thigh.

⑤ Say STAY and slide your hand off your dog's thigh, and then off her collar.

Note: The SIT-STAY and the DOWN-STAY are introduced in the next two lessons.

⑥ Stand up and step away from your dog gradually, repeating STAY to remind her to be still.

Note: Once your dog understands this direction, you can use it while brushing her. Initially, hold your left hand on her thigh/belly as you remind her to STAND and STAY.

SIT-STAY

SIT-STAY is not a complicated direction provided you progress through the lessons slowly. Nothing is more confusing or frustrating to a dog than to be taught to SIT-STAY one day in the quiet of your home and then immediately be expected to perform with company or in public. Instead, practice the following exercises in a low-distraction space, twice a day for ten minutes per session. Work inside for one to two weeks, depending on your dog's progress.

Teach Your Dog to Stay Sitting

1 Slide your dog's collar up between her ears or hold the chin ring of the head collar to the side of her face.

2 Instruct your dog to SIT and stand with your heel at your dog's paws. Hold the lead above her head, hip level, taut not tight. Keep your body upright and calm.

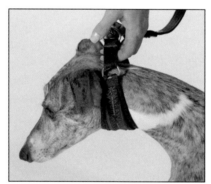

3 Give the STAY direction with a flat palm.

CONTINUED ON NEXT PAGE

④ Pivot in front of your dog and pause for three seconds. Repeat twice.

⑤ Introduce motion distractions: march in place, hop up and down, swirl your arm. Repeat the sequence three times for ten seconds each time.

⑥ Return to her side (with your feet in front of her paws) and release her with OKAY!

⑦ Introduce sound distractions. Moo like a cow, bark like a dog, meow like a kitten. Repeat twice.

Note: *Do not stare at your dog while you're in front of her—she'll perceive it as an invitation to play or as a threat. Instead, look at her ears.*

TIP

Can I remind my dog to STAY more than once?
Absolutely! There are two commands that you can repeat to remind your dog to continue on: STAY and HEEL.

Increase the Distractions

After practicing this direction in your home, you can gradually introduce STAY in more distracting environments. Go at a pace at which your dog feels comfortable: If she breaks consistently, you're going too quickly.

Use the 3-D guideline to increase distractions:

D	Element	Ideas
Duration	Time	Vary the time to pique interest.
Distraction	Motion and various sounds	Start with your movement, and then progress from controlled distractions to real-life situations.
Distance	Length from your dog's side	Move out a couple of feet at a time. Vary your angle, too. If your dog breaks repeatedly, go back a step to rebuild her success rate.

If your dog breaks, calmly reposition her by gently lifting up on her leash and squeezing her waist pressure point. Get as close to the original space in which you left her as possible. Remind her to STAY, and move closer if she fidgets.

If your dog breaks and moves away from the place you left her, calmly go to her and lead her back. Reposition her and reinstruct STAY. Remain close to reestablish her success rate.

TIP

Stay calm while teaching this lesson. Human frustration often creates tension for dogs and makes it even harder for them to stay still.

DOWN-STAY

To teach your dog a DOWN-STAY, she must be comfortable going into a DOWN position. If she's not, refer to page 93 and work on that lesson first.

Teach DOWN-STAY

1 Command STAY and stand very tall at your dog's side, with your toes in line with her toes. If she jumps right up, plant your left foot on her leash so that she feels tension when she tries to stand. If necessary, use the pressure point located between her shoulder blades to reposition her.

2 Make movements and sounds while standing at her side, and then pivot in front of her and repeat the sequence listed in the SIT-STAY section.

Once your dog has mastered the commands in this chapter, use them throughout the day to communicate with her. Practice a ten- to fifteen-minute lesson in which you fit each direction into an unpredictable routine. Introduce other distractions to make it lively, challenging, and interesting for both of you.

Make Medleys Fun and Effective

- Play music or be goofy to make it more fun.
- Involve friends and family members.
- Teach someone else how to direct your dog.
- Practice around increasingly greater distractions.

Use your directional commands to communicate with your dog throughout the day.

- Use SIT-STAY before dinner or pats.
- Use HEEL when walking through town.
- Use DOWN-STAY to urge your dog to relax with visitors.

The Invisible Leash

If your dog can control himself while he's off-leash, you have even more freedom and more opportunities to have fun together. Off-leash training gives you a companion who will choose to respond to your direction over distractions, one who will listen to you reliably and choose to follow your direction.

The transition from on-leash to off-leash control takes patience and time, and it means constantly reading your dog and being aware that your dog is also reading you. Because you have relied on the leash to communicate and reinforce your direction, its removal can be disorienting for both of you. For this reason alone, your off-leash goal will be a gradual progression, incorporating different types of leashes, and a blend of on-leash and off-leash exercises, until you are both confident in each other's responses. To have control, you must look like a leader, a team captain—confident, self-assured, and with a plan in mind. Only then will your dog trust your judgment.

Be sure to master the leash-training techniques in chapter 6 before you begin the exercises in this chapter. Of course, while this chapter is about the goal of off-leash training, you should continue to use some sort of containment during the process, especially when you are near a road or community. Throughout this chapter I will refer to leashes and other tools that can help you in your off-lead aspirations, and I will touch upon exactly when you can trust your direction without a leash. Find out how to get there in the pages ahead.

Practice Paying Attention

One of the most important qualities of an off-leash dog is that he focuses on you above all other distractions. If a bike, a rabbit, or another dog whizzes by and you call, your direction comes first.

If you were on a team, you wouldn't look to anyone but your team captain for instruction. That same devotion from your dog is within your grasp. The first step is to confirm his focus by practicing attention exercises on-leash.

Attention, Please

Ask someone to help you with this exercise.

1. Instruct your dog to HEEL and stand calmly. Have your helper approach you from the side clapping her hands, but not looking to or calling your dog.

2. The moment you see that your dog is more focused on the distraction than on you, call his name and step quickly in the opposite direction.

   Your dog will either follow you or he won't. If he doesn't, give his leash a quick tug as you move away from him.

3. Repeat the process until your dog is more focused on you than on the distraction.

4. Now, ask the person to approach with a more alluring distraction, like a sandwich. Repeat steps 1-3.

5. Continue to up the distractions, gradually increasing the level of the difficulty as you go: noise makers, other pets, etc.

TIP

Initially practice your lessons in an enclosed area or on a long line. When you start off-leash training, your dog may turn into a comedian and bound away from you just for fun, so keep it safe until he's reliable.

Heading Out into the Real World

Now you're ready to take this exercise into the real world. List your dog's top three distractions: things you may run into day to day. Here's a sample list:

- Other dogs
- Bicyclists or joggers
- Birds or squirrels

Now go out and find these things.

1. Line your dog up so that you are standing perpendicular to him. The temptations will be to your dog's left.

2. When he is clearly more focused on the distraction than on you, call his name and take a giant side step to the right.

3. Did he follow? YES!!! If he did not, register your existence by issuing a quick tug; then go back and present the choice again.

4. Continue to expose him to distractions until he learns to check in with you upon their sighting.

TIP

Repeating this exercise will help you establish a pattern of noting your dog's focus, which is especially important for off-lead work. Your dog must trust and follow your directions above all else that is going on around him. If you catch his attention wandering at any time, do a quick side-step reminder to get him back on track!

Hands-Free Control with a Short Lead

Using a short lead is an ideal way to make a smooth and nonconfrontational transition from on-leash to off-leash. Simply unclipping your leash one day may leave you feeling out of control, while at the same time giving your dog too much freedom too fast.

Letting Go of the Leash, Almost

The simple addition of a short lead weighs on your dog's collar, which serves as a reminder, and also enables you to slowly transition to hands-free exercises without having to ditch the leash entirely. Without it you might find yourself leaping or grabbing at your dog's collar to redirect him—especially if he's in danger. This is not good form. Impulsive movements on your part will frighten your dog and ensure a lack of off-leash trust.

Use the short lead around your home, directing your dog with simple cues like SIT, DOWN, STAY, and COME. If he responds, congratulations—if not, don't despair. Pick up your hand lead and guide him through it so he has faith in your direction. Avoid rushing outside or into the public domain with only a short lead, as your lack of full control will cause you to worry and be more reactive. Work on all your commands first, gaining confidence before you use your short lead in an open field or park. You can leave a short hand lead or an even smaller finger lead on your dog whenever you're supervising him. Think of it as giving you the ability to reach out and grasp your dog's hand when he gets confused or impulsive. If you want to do a spontaneous command medley (see page 107) or you need to direct your dog when someone comes into your home, you'll be able to do so without having to find a leash.

The other good thing about working on a short lead is that you can start an exercise while you're holding the leash and then drop it as your dog's focus improves. The slight weight on your dog's collar will be a reassuring reminder to him of your guidance.

TIP

It's so frustrating when my dog ignores me. I know I shouldn't, but I really feel like hitting him. What should I do?

Feeling like hitting is fine. Hitting isn't. Doing so would erode your relationship with your dog and diminish his off-lead trust. If you're really angry with him, walk away calmly. Remember, a graceful retreat is never disrespected.

In chapter 6, you learned that once your dog knows his commands, you can introduce the concept of NO into your lessons. NO, when paired with a tug of the leash, feeds your dog information about his performance. NO does not mean "bad dog"; it means "that response wasn't right—try again."

Redirect an Incorrect Response

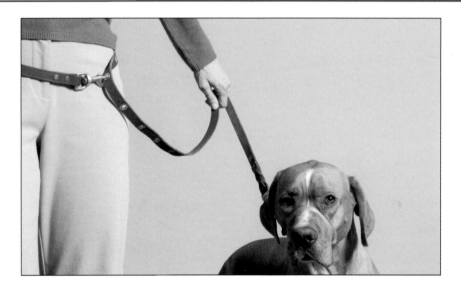

Command	Wrong Response	Correction
SIT	Ignores	Tug the lead and say NO. Wait two seconds for him to find the right response; if he doesn't, position him quickly. Praise him warmly if he cooperates.
DOWN	Ignores	Tug the lead and say NO. Wait two seconds for him to find the right response; if he doesn't, position him quickly. Praise him warmly if he cooperates.
HEEL	Lunges or veers	Quickly tug the leash and say NO. Redirect him with HEEL, and praise him for following along.
WAIT	Ignores	Tug him back behind you with a NO and reissue the direction WAIT. Repeat until he cooperates.
COME	Doesn't look to you when called	Say NO and tug the leash. When he does come, say YES and cheer him on.
COME	Veers away or races by	Cheer him on as he's coming toward you. If he races by, tug the leash and say NO! Repeat COME and praise him when he cooperates.
COME	Doesn't stop for the reconnection	Say NO and tug the leash. When he nears you, praise him.

TIP

Follow the two-second rule: wait two seconds for your dog to respond before you say NO.

When Your Dog Breaks

When your dog breaks a STAY command or bolts from you, stop for a minute to consider the motivation for his behavior. There are times when a correction is not appropriate—if, for example, he broke a SIT-STAY because he was moving to get out of the way of a cyclist or a car.

Your dog will break a direction for one of five reasons. The following table outlines those reasons, what each one looks like, and what your ideal response to each should be.

Reason for Break	Body Language	Your Response	Comments
Confusion/fear	Lowered posture, not moving or slinking away; stands there waiting for another direction from you	No eye contact, gently reposition, do not interact, stay close; simplify the exercise	When a dog breaks because he's confused, he often stands there waiting for another direction from you. Don't look at your dog or correct him. Calmly command him from a distance or, if necessary, go to him and reposition him.
Startled	Quick jumps, body oriented toward sound/stimulus	Instruct back into position; approach calmly and reposition only if necessary	People get startled, dogs get startled. Stay calm as you reposition your dog to show him that all is okay with the world.
Separation anxiety	Tail and head lowered, moving toward you	Don't touch, avoid eye contact, gently reposition, remain at dog's side, decrease difficulty of exercise	This dog is overwhelmed. He wants to be near you for reassurance. Do not shout at or correct him, as this will increase his level of anxiety. Calmly return him to his place and stay nearby. Gradually increase your distance while he's on-leash.
Defiance	Racing away, a quick stare over his shoulder	Lower your head, walk calmly and quickly to your dog's side, lift the leash or hook your finger under his collar, tug firmly, say NO, and return to position. Use a training collar to reinforce the concept of NO.	This dog has no interest in following your direction. Strong-minded and self-assured, he just leaves, most likely when a new element is introduced: either a high-level distraction like a person or a dog, or a new location.
Testing	Walking away, continually checking in with you visually	Lower your head; go to dog calmly, and step on his leash. Return him to the original position without interaction. Instruct STAY and make the exercise simpler.	This response is often accompanied with a play bow; it is a sign of your dog's tension at your expectation. Simplify your request and correct your dog's mischief with a NO and a leash tug.

TIP

When a dog breaks a command, it is often because you've increased the difficulty of the exercise before he's ready to take on the challenge. Look at everything from your dog's perspective; if you're in a new location, decrease your expectation and distance initially.

If you haven't worked through the exercises in chapter 6, where the command COME is intro-duced, flip there now and make sure your dog understands that COME means together and happy, not apart and stressed.

Before working on your off-leash goals, review the three steps of COME, gradually introducing greater distances between you and your dog.

NAME ASSOCIATION

During the day, call out your dog's name. Do so when you're standing apart from your dog, and praise him for looking to you. If he ignores you, call out his name as you shake a treat cup. He may be ignoring you because you've used his name in discouragement or repeated it often with a negative consequence (such as medication or isolation). It's not too late to reverse this trend. Your goal is to excite your dog, so say his name cheerfully and with plenty of enthusiasm.

RECONNECTION

When your dog hears the word COME, you want him to think immediately of being near you. When he isn't near you and he hears this command, he should immediately want to run over to you to reconnect. To establish this sense of urgency and fun, act up when you call to him. Say COME and then step back or run away from him or even run and hide. Do this exercise in the house where there are few distractions. Praise him a lot when he gets to your side and reward him with hugs, treats, or a toy. Mix up the rewards so he'll never know what to expect.

COMING FROM A DISTANCE

Outside also stress that your reconnection is the most important part of this direction. As your dog comes to you from a distance, encourage him to slow down and stop when he nears you, and then reward and touch him. This way he'll know that the COME is complete when you're physically reconnecting with him.

Know When to Trust Your Dog to COME

The hardest part of COME is knowing when you can trust your dog—you should feel it. It's never a smooth road in the beginning; some days you will get a quick and happy response, others will feel more like your first day of training. Just remember that frustration is a sign of weakness and you'll lose your dog's respect. When you're first testing your level of control, bring your dog to an enclosed area. Be calm and relaxed, and don't be afraid to back track to an early phase of training. If you're at all unsure, use the long line exercise described on page 99.

When letting your dog romp off-leash for the first time, you're nerves will be the hardest thing to control. Before you begin:

- Place treats in your pocket or snack pack, and bring a clicker if you're using one in your dog's training.

- Bring several of your dog's favorite toys, such as Frisbees or balls.

- Bring your long line just in case your dog is not cooperative.

- Walk your dog or exercise him with another dog to take the edge off his excitability.

- Read over the sections on the off-leash COME.

- Relax. The more confident you seem, the more your dog will want to stay around you.

TIP

My dog comes well but often runs right by, crashes into me, or plays keep away. What should I do?

Mr. Funny. You need to work on the reconnection exercises on page 98 to teach him that the COME command means that you're together: the equivalent of a human huddle, with the team coming together to establish a sense of unity.

Do not get in the habit of calling your dog every thirty seconds. That's one way to ensure that he'll ignore you. Use other directions to get his attention, like NAME, LET'S GO, INSIDE, or BALL. For example, when you need to turn around or head back to the house call out INSIDE or LET'S GO to highlight your movement, rather than saying COME. Call him to you no more than twice when you're walking. Initially end each exercise with a release so that your dog doesn't see COME as the end to your fun.

Alternative to COME

Try this routine while out on a walk or playing with your dog.

1 Call out your dog's name as you turn in the opposite direction.

2 Run a few paces away from him. If he's following, cheer him on!

3 Turn to face him and kneel down.

4 Hug him into you, reward him, and release him with OKAY, GO PLAY!

FAQ

What if he doesn't come?

Don't get upset—you'll only teach him to avoid you off-leash. Instead, take out the treat cup or a toy and begin to play all by yourself or pretend to eat his treats. Do not look at or talk with him until you've re-leashed him. When he comes to investigate, gently take his collar and secure his long line. Review the above exercise, holding his long line as you run back.

Deal with Less-Than-Perfect Reactions to COME

A perfect response to COME doesn't happen overnight. Two reactions are common to many dogs when they're adjusting to off-leash freedom. Some go through one or the other; others go through both phases. Thinking of each reaction in human terms makes it more understandable.

Have We Met?

Your dog may give you a blank stare like he has no idea who you are. He's just showing signs of stress at having no leash to guide him and is testing his freedom. Follow these steps:

1 Lower your head to break the eye contact immediately.

2 Sit down, take out a favorite toy or treat cup, and begin to play with it or pretend to eat the treats yourself. Sometimes this works perfectly: if it does, gently take your dog's collar, say NO, and place him back on his leash.

3 If the above fails to impress your dog, try running away from him as you shake his cup or swing a stick playfully.

4 If all else fails, lower your head and walk sideways or backward toward your dog. Moving head-on is seen as confrontational.

5 Kneel down as you get close. Gently reach for his collar—do not be angry. Leave him on his long line and practice the exercise on the following page.

In a Minute

Think back to when you were seven years old and were called in for lunch. You really didn't hear your name being called the first ten times. Your dog will do the same thing. Be sympathetic to his reaction, but teach him that COME is not a choice.

1 When you get this look, your dog's tail will be wagging, and his expression will be playful. Then he'll turn back to whatever he was doing. When he does, say NO firmly.

2 If he looks back, throw your arms up in a cheer and call out his name. Then run in the opposite direction and/or play with a favorite toy or treat cup.

3 If you must, approach him calmly, and secure him to the leash.

4 Leave his long line on for one week. Each time he gives you the "look," tug the leash and say NO. Praise his cooperation.

Work Around Distractions

It's common for your dog to be more distracted when you're practicing commands in public. Don't be discouraged or get frustrated. Your dog will sense this and will be less likely to cooperate. Instead, set up situations to teach him to focus on you even *more*. Practice these exercises on a short leash; if you anticipate his impulses will triumph, let him drag his leash so you're able to interfere if he gets too distracted. Repeat the exercises below until your dog focuses on you above all else.

Distraction Exercises

Lay distractions on the floor in your living room. Try an open potato chip bag, a used wrapper, or a paper towel. Bring your dog into the room on his leash and training collar. Tug the leash (if necessary) and say NO if he focuses more on the object than on you (review the exercise on page 84).

Next, increase the level of floor distractions. Add some bits of food or another pet. Work through the commands SIT, DOWN, HEEL, and COME, correcting any lack of focus with the command NO. Redirect your dog if necessary, and praise him for his attention.

Now take these same distractions outside. Work in a familiar environment initially, gradually increasing the level of distractions as you did inside. Eventually work in environments that are unfamiliar, continuing to lay down an obstacle course of temptations for your dog. Each time he focuses intensely on an object, say NO and redirect him. Praise all cooperation.

Now you're ready to take on the world. Think of every distraction as you did when you set up distractions in chapter 6 and practiced your exercises around them. Watch your dog's ears to determine his focus: If they're pricked and forward, his attention is rooted on the distraction. If they're flickering back, he's aware of the distraction but also attuned to you. If you wonder where his focus is, side step to the right—does his head follow you, or is his focus elsewhere?

If you're walking your dog at HEEL and he's suddenly distracted by a jogger or bicyclist, take a giant step to the right and remind HEEL. If he follows you, praise him; if not, tug his collar or the leash. (Please always leave a leash attached if you're near a roadway.)

Is your dog enchanted by a scent? Is he dying to mark every tree? Unless you'd like to mark along with him, set the rhythm of the walk, leaving all marking opportunities for closer to your home. Let his leash go slack and step away from him. Does he follow? If not, say NO as you tug the leash, then remind HEEL and continue walking, or remind STAY if you're standing still.

City streets are littered with tasty bits of garbage. The smells will intoxicate your dog. If he's more enticed by the smells than by your direction, tug the collar/leash quickly and say NO. Reissue your original direction and praise his cooperation.

Train with a Retractable Leash

Another option in your march toward off-leash cooperation is a retractable leash; however, it should never be used in a crowd or near a road. When used in an open environment, it allows your dog the freedom to explore, while still allowing you to reinforce your direction. As a training tool, you can use it informally during walks to reinforce the following commands.

Command	Response
NAME	Call out your dog's name enthusiastically. If he looks at you, praise him. That's all that is required—just a glance. If he ignores you, tug his leash, say NO, and then praise him once you have his attention.
WAIT	Use WAIT to teach your dog to stop at a distance. Command your dog to stop when he is three feet in front of you. If your dog continues forward, snap the leash and say NO, WAIT. Praise his focus immediately. Increase your distance to six feet, eight feet, twelve feet, sixteen feet, and twenty-six feet.
SIT-STAY	Use a retractable leash to increase your distance control. Increase your distance slowly.
HEEL	Use this command to call your dog back to your side. Call out his name and then command HEEL as you slap your leg. Praise your dog as he responds, and then walk a short distance before you stop to release him.
NO	Whenever your dog is focusing on something he shouldn't be, call his name and run in the other direction, if possible. If he ignores you, snap the leash and say NO. Immediately refocus his attention with a toy, a stick, or a command.

Work on a Ten-Foot Security Line

You can use your security line to vary the flow of your exercises and strengthen your dog's reliability with the STAY command. This exercise flows from a short lead series and will sharpen your dog's focus as he will initially consider his freedom once the short lead is removed. An impulse to break will be self-corrected as he hits the end of the lead. By letting this lead system correct your dog and weighing in only to reinforce cooperation, your dog will learn to focus on your direction over the weight of the leash.

Distance Control

Tie a ten-foot line to a tree or post and secure all knots. Leave the line on the ground and follow this sequence:

1. Warm up with five minutes of regular on-leash practice.

2. Stop your dog next to the tree line and discreetly attach it to his buckle collar. Remove his regular leash and place it on the ground in front of him. Keep your hands free.

3. Command STAY and walk ten feet away. Extend your distance as your dog gains control. Run your fingers through your hair and swing your arms gently back and forth to emphasize that he is off-leash.

4. As your dog improves, practice an out-of-sight SIT-STAY. Practice DOWN from a SIT-STAY. You can also practice the command COME, but never call it from a distance greater than the line will reach.

Note: If your dog darts for a quick getaway, wait until he is about to hit the end of the line before you shout NO. Return him to the original position and repeat the exercise at a closer range.

Use a Long Line

You can use your long line outside as a training tool when you're supervising your dog's freedom. Attach the line and let him roam free as you keep a watchful eye. Engage him by playing with a stick or a ball, and investigate your surroundings together. Avoid overcommanding; just hang out and enjoy some free time together. Every five minutes, position yourself near the line and issue a command enthusiastically.

WAIT

Command your dog to stop in his tracks, varying the distance between you. All he must do when he hears this command is stop. If he chooses to sit or come back to you, do not discourage him, but it is not a requirement.

WAIT means stop—praise him for that. If he ignores the direction, quickly step on the line and say NO. When he is forced to stop, say WAIT and praise his forced cooperation.

NAME

This command directs your dog to stop, turn around, and make eye contact with you. He does not need to come or stay; he simply needs to check in. If he does, throw your arms up in praise. If he ignores you, step on the leash and say NO. Say his name again as you run a short distance in the opposite direction or toss your head.

COME

COME is the canine equivalent of huddle. It is the ultimate command of reconnection. Make sure that you've mastered WAIT and NAME before putting it all together with this one. Initially, call out your dog's name while standing near the long line. If he doesn't listen, step on the line and say NO. When he looks at you, praise him generously and say COME as you step back or dart in the opposite direction. Kneel and open your arms to welcome him and enforce the actual reconnection. If he keeps running, step on the line and say NO as he reaches the end. Say COME again and reel or welcome him in when he gets to you.

Emergency DOWN

This exercise can be a real lifesaver—it gets your dog to drop like a shot. The reaction is ancestral—the leader of a wolf pack makes a sound that sends the whole pack to the den for cover. Your dog must DOWN comfortably (see page 93) before you can start practicing this exercise. In the beginning, it can be a little confusing, so be patient and positive throughout the training process.

Out-of-the-Blue DOWN

1 While standing next to your unsuspecting dog, suddenly command DOWN in a life-threatening tone (the type of tone you would use if a loved one were about to walk off a cliff). Point toward the ground as you do so.

2 Kneel down quickly and help your dog down if he looks confused. To reinforce the point, act like you're being bombed, too.

CONTINUED ON NEXT PAGE

3 When your dog begins to catch on and act independently, extend your distance from him. Someday, this exercise could halt a treacherous situation or save your dog's life—for instance, if you were ever separated by a road and his safety were threatened by an oncoming vehicle.

Note: *This is a very stressful exercise. Practice only two emergency DOWNs a day.*

TIP

It's all a mind game at this stage. You must be positive, structured, and mentally tough. You're the leader—now's the time to show it. Your dog's anticipating your behavior as you try to anticipate his. Stand tall, command confidently, and don't be afraid to be goofy and have a little fun.

Eventually you will come to a place with your dog where you'll notice that his cooperation is a given, no commands required. This is a wonderful sign of a dog who has internalized your direction to the point that he hears it automatically and in your absence. You need to be very consistent to get to this level. If your dog is at all uncertain about what he should do, he is not ready for this step.

Recognize Default Behavior

Here are some telltale default behaviors:

- He stops automatically at the door and waits for your permission to go.
- He walks next to you without being told to HEEL.
- He lies down automatically at mealtimes.
- He knows to lie down under your chair or at your side when out in public.
- He circles back and checks in with you while you're hiking, no COME necessary.

Don't forget to praise his cooperation at these times!

In some instances, you can encourage default behavior. When you approach a door, pause; if your dog doesn't stop with you, tug the leash gently and say NO. If he knows the direction, you will notice that he steps back in an effort to contain himself. If he continues, he doesn't know the direction well enough to respond without a verbal cue. Keep practicing!

Has your dog internalized walking near you? Take him out on his leash and begin your normal routine without commanding HEEL. Does he pull ahead or sniff around?

If so, tug the leash and say NO. Does he step back to your side? If so, praise and reward him. If not, you'll need to continue with your verbal commands for a bit longer.

When you sit down with company or when you're in town, does your dog sit or lie down under you without being told? If so, praise him. If not, tug the leash, say NO, and remind him of your expectations.

chapter 8

Socialization Plus

One of the most valuable things you can do with your dog is to socialize her *a lot!* The more exposure she has to different people, places, surfaces, and settings, the more comfortable she will be in your world. And the earlier you start, the more easily she will adapt to a wide variety of experiences. At around four months of age, a puppy develops a sense of "stimulus memory," which greatly limits her openness to new experiences. Whenever possible expose your puppy to new stimulus, inoculated dogs, and safe, controlled situations. This is not to say that an older dog won't tolerate new stimuli; it's just that she may be more wary or defensive in unfamiliar situations. These reactions are not bad or abnormal—fear/defensiveness is nothing more than a lack of exposure and trust in your direction. In the previous chapters we discuss communication and training as steps to help you organize your dog's experience. As you venture out use any and all familiar commands in order to help your dog/puppy feel safe and to normalize new experiences.

People

Your dog will pick up many cues from you when meeting new people. If you're uncomfortable with children, your dog will be, too. If men in uniform make you tense, you'll send that message right down the leash. Be mindful of this: your dog will convey her emotions differently. Whereas you probably wouldn't bite a small child who was crowding you, your dog might.

A better plan is to contain your concerns and expose your dog to new people in a controlled setting to ensure that she will be accepting and remain calm.

Exercise and feed your dog before venturing out. Place her in a training collar (see pages 32–34) and leash, and use familiar words to guide her and make her feel safe. HEEL, WAIT, and STAY are three top favorites:

- HEEL reminds your dog to pause and await further instruction.
- WAIT instructs your dog to stand behind you, not in front.
- STAY lets your dog know that you're in control and that the best action is to be still.

Your dog's first reactions to strangers will be pronounced. Excitement is the norm. Calm handling sets the best example, and your dog will relax the more she is exposed. If her reaction is stressed use the table below to determine if she is being dominant aggressive or is fearful. Watch for these signs:

Body	Fearful	Dominant/Aggressive
Eye contact	Eyes dart back and forth; constantly avoiding focus	Stares at the stranger; lacks trust in their intent
Body language	Body pulled way back in fear	Leaned forward in a protective stance; her focus is not on your reaction
Tail	Down low under the belly or arched high on alert; she is distressed	Arched above rump; still or short and rapid wags
Lips	Pulled back, facial and body tension	Pursed/growling

If you can't lessen the intensity of your dog's reactions within a few outings, call a professional trainer for guidance.

CHILDREN

If your dog is leery of children, introduce her to their activities and noise near a playground. Do not allow children to approach you, especially if you don't know them! Gradually walk closer and sit quietly with your dog until she is more familiar. Use a Gentle Leader if the fear does not go away. Read your dog's signals—lip licking and pulling away are signs that she's had enough.

THE ELDERLY

Older people may present a concern for your dog. Our odor changes as we age, and we have less voluntary muscle control. Teach your dog to stay at your heel (using the directions HEEL and WAIT) and introduce older people by taking their hands in yours and letting your dog sniff them together.

GENDER

If your dog is unaccustomed to men, she may grow up leery of them, especially if her only exposure to them has been brief and noninteractive (such as with mailmen and landscapers). To prevent this, bring her out as often as possible and introduce her to men of all ages. Encourage a DOWN-STAY and ask that the man feed her a favorite treat that you've brought along.

The same can be said for a dog raised in a home where women are absent. Once your dog is comfortable greeting members of the opposite sex, teach her GO SAY HELLO by pointing (page 143) to the new person and let her approach them on her own.

CONTINUED ON NEXT PAGE

SIZES

People come in many sizes and shapes. Often a trip to the city or a busy town will help condition your dog to the variety.

RACES

Dogs are not racist, but they do note changes in skin coloration and odor. If your community is not integrated, bring your dog into environments where she will have ample exposure to people of every race. Use a SIT-STAY and treats to help her make the link that everyone is a friend. If you get a home delivery from a person of a different race, use that as a time to improve your dog's greeting skills as well as to socialize her to people of different ethnicities.

PEOPLE WITH SPORTING EQUIPMENT

Although you might know a family member geared up for sporting play, your dog may not. Where vision is our strongest sense, it is a dog's weakest. Visual novelties often send a dog's senses into a spin, and the reaction may be extreme. Try to resist soothing your dog when she's agitated as doing so conveys concern, not confidence. Use the direction HEEL and walk around the outside perimeter of a sporting event with her. If sporting gear is to be worn around your home, lay each piece of it on the floor and spend time exploring it with your dog, showing her how to "view it" with her nose.

UNIFORMS

From police officers to mail carriers, many dogs have an innate dislike of anyone who doesn't dress down. Although the temptation may be to tense up or to jolly beyond your dog's comfort zone, there is an appropriate way to react to ensure that your dog views these people just like anyone else. First, pass these people by, or practice a lesson when the mail carrier makes a delivery without acknowledging her. Repeat this as often as necessary until your dog is less reactive. Next, use the command HEEL to walk over to the person, and ask your dog to SIT-STAY before greeting. Ask the person to help you offer your dog treats, holding that person's hand in yours to convey your mutual respect.

COSTUMES

Costumes and large human-form decorations, especially around Halloween and at parades, can be very frightening to a dog. The best way to preempt your dog's fear is to lay the object or outfit on the floor and investigate it with her: act like another dog and sniff it together. When you meet a person in disguise, use HEEL if you're moving and STAY if you're not. Ignore your dog's reactions, holding the leash comfortably until she calms down.

PEOPLE HOLDING/CARRYING EQUIPMENT OR OTHER OBJECTS

When a person is carrying an object, she can suddenly look monstrous to a dog—even if that person is you. If the object is motorized, it can add another dimension of caution. If your dog is caught off guard, her impulse to protect or run in fear may lead to hazardous reactions. To prepare her, keep her on-leash when people are working near your home; use SIT-STAY to help her contain her initial reaction and focus on you. If you have purchased or plan to use an object that might be alarming, lay it on the floor in advance and investigate it together.

Places

Going on new adventures can do a world of good for your relationship with your dog if you structure them well. Your dog will put a lot of pride in your worldliness and your ability to lead her safely into new, uncharted territories. You look big and bold, while she's still a bit unsure. Bring your dog with you as often as possible, and expose her to many enriching environments, remembering that she sees new places with her nose. Whenever possible, let her sniff for a few moments to help calm her.

BUSY PARKING LOT

A good place to expose your dog to increasingly greater distractions is a supermarket parking lot. Start at the periphery, away from much of the distraction. Work through some of your early SIT-STAY and HEEL lessons. Gradually move closer to the market as your dog's focus improves.

CITY VS. COUNTRY

Whether you live in the city or the country, the opposite location can be shocking. It's ideal if you can expose your dog to the different setting at a young age. Keep a city dog on a long leash and let her sniff the country to her heart's content, but keep a country dog at your side on leash, as the city noises will easily overwhelm her.

OFFICE

If you have control over your work environment, set up a corner in it for your dog with a mat, toys, chews, and a secured leash if she can't sit still initially. Give her attention for being calm, and work through her initial anxieties when the office is free of people or the store is closed.

OTHER PEOPLE'S HOMES

Many dogs pee shortly after being brought into someone else's home. Often surprising to humans, it makes complete sense from a dog's perspective: new situations make her uneasy, and urinating spreads her scent, making her feel more at home. Guide your dog into new homes, encouraging WAIT and OKAY through all doorways, and give her a familiar mat and bone to occupy her by your side.

TOWN

Going to town is an exciting experience, especially if your dog has been cooped up all day or is undersocialized. Letting her have the leash and pull you left and right is wrong. It's disruptive to other people, overwhelming to your dog, and not enjoyable for you. Using your commands (from previous chapters) and structuring the experience from the beginning can make the difference between a positive town adventure and chaotic one.

TIP

If, while strolling, you'd like to stop at a cafe or outdoor deli, fold the leash up neatly and sit on it, giving your dog just enough freedom to lie comfortably. If you are able, lead your dog under your legs or table, combining a new direction with an old one: UNDER-DOWN.

Other Dogs

Socializing your dog with other dogs can be an exciting experience. The key is to understand how much your dog depends on your body language to communicate to her and make her feel safe. In return, you'll need to understand hers. When first meeting each other, dogs must determine a few things: age, sex, and relative status. For two or more dogs to play comfortably together, they must establish a social hierarchy. Here's a guideline of introductions, what to expect, and when to interfere.

Allow Them to Introduce Themselves

The best introductions are made either on a loose lead, such as a long line, or off-leash: dogs need space to check each other out and communicate in their own private language. Human tensions and interference will confuse them and may skew their reactions. Consider taking the dogs to a field or a park to meet. Although tensions may arise initially, when left to their own devices they will work it out.

When dogs greet

- They approach one another from the side;
- They often circle, sometimes with the hair on their backs raised, to determine who will be in charge;
- They may flash their teeth, snarl, or jump on each other; all signs of normal interactions in their attempts to get along.

When they've finished with the initial introduction, you may notice that they lower themselves into a submissive posture to play, grab a stick or a toy, or begin sniffing and marking the surrounding location.

Puppies are a special case. Puppies up to six months of age don't act like other dogs and are nurtured and forgiven for many "bad" behaviors for which an older dog would be corrected, such as stealing a toy or biting. They often approach straight on, in a lowered, submissive posture. Piddling is a sign of respect. If a dog has not been socialized well with puppies, she may consider their chaotic behavior threatening and attack or avoid them.

Know When to Interfere

If both dogs are trying to dominate one another and their vocalizations are escalating to the point of concern, you may separate them calmly. Do not shout or get physical, as your involvement will be seen as confrontational and will fuel their aggression. Instead, spray them with water or a blaster.

You may also, with another person to handle the second dog, pull them apart using their long lines by grasping the base of their tails forcefully. Pull them up and away from each other.

FAQ

My dog is comfortable meeting new dogs off-leash, but on-leash, it's a different story: she gets vicious, and I literally have to drag her away. How do I keep this from happening?

This is a common reaction. Off-leash, your dog can body posture freely with other dogs in their mutual efforts to get to know one other. On-leash, your efforts to "hold" her throw her body into an unnaturally defensive stance. If the other dog is on-leash, too, expect confusion all around.

Other Animals

Consider other animals your dog may see on your walks or visits together. Make a master list, decide on your plans of action for each—on-leash or off—and share your ideas with everyone involved in your dog's care. If you are caught unaware, your reaction may be impulsive and may actually encourage a more exaggerated response from your dog the next time around.

First, make a list of all the animals you might encounter: cats, squirrels, rabbits, ducks, geese, farm animals, guinea pigs, and so on. Include indoor pets as well as wild critters your dog might see outdoors.

The goal when you and your dog see these animals together is for your dog to pay more attention to you than to the animal. When you tell your dog WAIT, HEEL, or COME, she will heed your direction above her impulse to chase the creature. Reaching this level of focus takes a high level of maturity and training, but the foundations of such respect should start today. Each time your dog is more focused on the animal than on you, step away from her and call her name. Does she follow you? If not, tug her leash and say NO. Repeat this process as often as necessary to get her attention.

FAQ

What about when we are approached? What sets my dog off is not an animal running away, but another dog chasing us. She gets aggressive and pulls on the leash, when otherwise she's playful.

The leash is putting her body in a compromised pose, which is aggravating to say the least. A dog running at you is also an overwhelming sight. Combining these creates a fight-or-flight reaction, and since flight is out of the question, your dog must hunker down. Teach her a strong heel and review the attention exercise on page 91. When the other dog approaches, remind your dog to HEEL and move quickly out of what this dog perceives as his territory. The other dog will refrain from attack, saving his energies for a more formidable foe.

Other directions that are useful to condition your dog toward a greater tolerance for other animals are outlined in the following table:

Command	Response
HEEL	Your dog must walk a step behind you when you're passing or surrounded by live distractions.
WAIT	This command tells your dog to stop, on-leash or off, and contain her impulses until you release her with OKAY.
SIT-STAY	This second-level containment skill encourages focus and can be paired with bracing (see page 79) to help your dog ground herself when she's overexcited.
DOWN	This is a difficult containment exercise, but once your dog respects it, it's a marvelous way to help her relax when stimulated. An ideal time to practice this skill would be when you're visiting a home where animals abound.
COME	Although full off-leash focus on this direction is not expected before social maturity (a year to two years), it's a skill to continue working on. If your dog is not reliable, keep her on a long line, and if she's entranced by another animal, call her name as you move quickly in the opposite direction.

TIP

It's very hard for your dog to contain her chasing impulse—it's like asking a person not to chase a one hundred dollar bill floating by in the wind. Give your dog some suitable "game" alternatives (see chapter 9), and take her to an enclosed area where you can let her chase and play without interference.

Things

Condition your dog to household objects that she doesn't see every day—balloons, strollers, grocery carts, umbrellas, garden hoses, and so on. Although a floating balloon heralds a celebration to you, your dog may be caught off guard by the strange sight. Dogs in this state of alert are known to bark, look fearful, or displace their confusion onto a person or object by snapping or jumping.

Set-Up Situations

If your dog is spooked, find her Red Zone—the distance from the object at which she feels comfortable—and work with her there. To condition your dog to new objects, follow these steps:

1. At an unstressful time, place the foreign object in the middle of the floor.
2. Walk your dog by it without seeming to pay attention to it or to her reaction.

   If it makes her nervous, increase your distance from the object.
3. Walk by repeatedly until she is less reactive.

4. Let her leash drop, and go up to the object and investigate it as if you were another dog.

   Do not force your dog to follow you—just let her observe you.
5. When she approaches the object, stay very calm. Pet her after she relaxes. Feed her food rewards if she will take them.

Objects that move, like grocery carts and wheelchairs, can be particularly startling to a dog. Remind HEEL and walk your dog at a gradually diminishing distance from the moving object until she feels more comfortable. Investigate the object together while it's still.

Objects that have unfamiliar shapes or that suddenly change from one shape to another can generate a strong startle response in a dog. The best way to integrate the object into your dog's world is to leave it out for several days. Leave treats on or by it, and investigate the object yourself to show both comfort and confidence.

Many dogs are uncomfortable walking on or near grates. They are wary of both the grate's crossed pattern and its dark spaces; dogs do not have depth perception like humans do. If you soothe or drag your dog over to a grate, you may create a lifelong phobia. Instead, slow it down. Stand on or near the grate yourself and remain quiet until your dog approaches. Then look at her calmly and reward her.

Surfaces

Dogs are sensitive to surfaces like gravel, ice, pavement, and tile to varying degrees until they are conditioned to them. Your dog depends on her equilibrium and balance in interpreting her surroundings. Pair that with her inability to reason a surface change, and the result is often a startle reaction when her ground surface changes suddenly. Be mindful of this when you're navigating with your dog, and take time to acclimate her to new surfaces using food, toys, patience, and praise.

Many dogs do not adjust well to hard, unforgiving surfaces—they offer nothing for their paws to grasp. If your past reaction to your wary dog has been to plead, placate, or drag her across such a surface, your attention has reinforced her fear. Be patient. Spread towels across the floor to provide a magic carpet; then downgrade to copier paper. Sit on the floor and offer treats when your dog ventures to be near you.

Tubs and sinks feel very unsafe to many dogs—especially those who don't like water. Again, it's the fear of nothing to grasp with their paws and the slippery feeling when they try to move. When you have to bathe your dog, lay a towel down or use a tub mat to help your dog feel more secure.

If your dog is surface sensitive, wooden stairs will undo her. Stairs throw off a dog's balance, and although she can readjust, the added loss of sure footing will not be received well. You have two options: carpet your stairs or gradually introduce your dog to walking up and down wooden ones as described on page 70.

Take a moment to look at stimulating environments from your dog's perspective: fast movements, human activity that is far more elevated than she's used to experiencing, and a sense of disconnection from you—especially when you're one of the participants. If bringing your dog with you to activities is new, don't expect a smooth transition. Your dog will need your help to maintain her sense of stability as you go from place to place.

Dogs are territorial by nature: if they lived in the wild, they would not travel outside a given zone, known as their territory. Within their zone, they'd know each tree, rock, and field intimately. Adapting to sudden changes in the world does not come naturally to them. And yet exposure and socialization is something they tolerate and enjoy; in turn, you can look courageous and brave since you'll be leading your dog into these situations. Make a list of stimulating activities or places that you are likely to experience with your dog—after-school games, parades, picnics, parks, train stations, etc.—and think about how you can prepare your dog for each of them.

- When you bring your dog to social activities, use WAIT at the car, and SIT-STAY and HEEL to teach her to stay by your side. If the opportunity arises to greet another person or dog, do so in a civilized manner: have your dog WAIT and then release her with GO SAY HELLO. When time is up, call her to HEEL.

- If you live near a train station, socialize your dog to the experience and teach her to stay clear of the tracks. Work with her at increasingly close distances to the platform, using HEEL and STAY to help organize her focus and contain her anxiety or excitability. To teach her to stay clear of the tracks, take her out when the train is set to arrive. As it pulls near, run away from the train shouting as though you've been hit by a bullet. Do not look at your dog while doing so. Repeat until your dog knows to run from the tracks.

- A veterinarian's office can be a super-stimulating place. The smells are familiar but often repellent. There are often multiple species to be found. And most dogs learn early on that they don't want to be there. Bring a familiar blanket and toys so that your dog has a more positive association. Have your dog WAIT at the door until she calms down. Spread her blanket underneath you in the waiting room and instruct your dog UNDER. Use STAY if she fidgets. When you go to the exam room, spread the blanket on the examination table, and use your words for familiarity and focus.

9

Games and Tricks

The best part of sharing life with a dog is the fun you'll have together. Although training and hard work seem to make up a large part of the early stages in your relationship, the real goal is mutual respect so that you can—at every golden opportunity from here on out—play.

There's no better way to bond with your dog than to integrate lessons into your day through play training. The right games and tricks will teach your dog that focusing on you is fun!

Runaway Come

You can use a treat cup or a clicker and treats to encourage your dog's motivation in the Runaway Come game. This game encourages a positive association to coming when called.

1 Stand five to ten feet from your dog; keep him on a long line if the space is not enclosed or if he's unfocused.

2 Call his name as you run away from him, shaking the treat cup if you're carrying one.

3 Turn to face your dog, treat, and hug him as you say COME! GOOD COME!

Add a twist: Call your dog's name as you duck out of sight. He'll learn to look for you when he can't see you.

Two-Ball Toss

This game will teach your dog many things: retrieving skills, focus, and, most important, that you're the one to watch. Start with two similar objects, such as two balls.

1 Get your dog excited about one object, and then toss it.

2 Praise his enthusiasm for chasing, and run back from him if he moves toward you.

3 Stop focusing on him right away.

4 Bring out the other object and play with it like it's the most important thing in the world, ignoring your dog. He'll want what you have. Continue to ignore him for ten seconds.

5 Suddenly notice him and encourage him to SIT or WAIT. Throw your object and praise him again.

6 Pick up the first ball that he's dropped and start over again from the top!

To make a treat cup, simply fill a cup that has a lid with a hole in it halfway with broken bits of your dog's favorite treats or cereal. Strategically place several of these cups around the house and shake them throughout the day as you call your dog's name. Once he associates the sound with pleasure, teach him the names of everyone in your home.

1. Start with two people (in this example, Robin and Sarah—their dog's name is Daisy) standing six feet apart.

2. Say DAISY.

3. When Daisy arrives, have Robin instruct her to SIT before giving her a treat.

4. Have Robin send Daisy back: DAISY, GO TO SARAH.

5. Sarah now repeats the calling sequence and, after treating, sends Daisy back to Robin.

6. Repeat this process five times.

As your dog catches onto the game, you may include other people and/or extend your distance or hide in between callings. This game is a great way to encourage enthusiastic COMES outdoors.

This game encourages following skills in young puppies and smaller breeds.

1 Tie a small toy/bone to one end of a leash.

2 Clip or tie the other end of the leash to your ankle.

3 Walk around. If your dog begins to tug hard at the toy/bone, simply unclip the lead from your ankle and secure it to an immovable object.

Swing Toss

This game is a great way to burn up your dog's excess energy. It can be played indoors or out.

1 Tie an empty bottle or hollow toy onto a five- to fifteen-foot rope.

2 Lace the opening of the bottle/toy with a creamy spread.

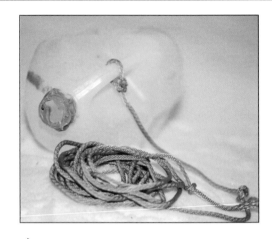

3 Swing the toy around you.

4 Run with the toy dragging behind you.

5 Toss the toy into the brush and wiggle it like a small animal.

Note: *If your dog tugs on it, tie the toy around a secure object and tug with him—not against him.*

This game is great for athletic dogs who've developed a habit of chasing interactively. Play it with one or more soda bottles or balls.

1. Kick one bottle or ball playfully near your dog.

2. When he alerts to you, kick the object for him to chase.

3. Immediately divert your attention to the other bottle or ball and repeat the pattern.

FAQ

What about tug of war and all-out wrestling?
These games convey the wrong message, teaching your dog to challenge and defend himself in opposition to you. Avoid these games in light of the many other options you have. If your dog loves to tug, tie a toy onto an immovable object, like a tree or a banister, and tug with him.

Sometimes the best tricks are the ones that your dog does spontaneously. Work with friends and family to come up with fun phrases to elicit natural responses.

1 IF YOU'RE HAPPY AND YOU KNOW IT WAG YOUR TAIL! Said in a fun, happy tone, this is a surefire winner.

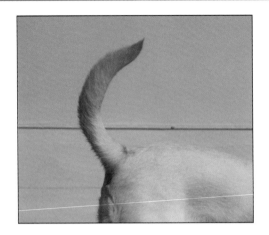

2 SAD PUPPY! When your dog lays a sleepy head on the floor or on your lap, it is quite endearing.

3 PUSH IT! When your dog noses an object or a toy, you can quickly expand it to a rolling game of ball, or even to closing an open cupboard.

Note: If you say appropriate commands as your dog naturally does different activities, he'll make the association between the word and the action, and you'll be able to direct him to repeat them anytime.

The easiest way to introduce this trick is simply to catch your dog in the act of stretching and say BOW. For a snappy signal, you can bow to your dog as he's stretching out. After five to ten stretch-BOW sequences, practice this routine to tie it all together:

1. Take your dog into a nondistracting environment. Bring irresistible treats.

2. Instruct STAND, holding your hand or finger under his belly.

3. Now lower the treat from your dog's nose to the ground as though you were luring him into a down position.

4. As your dog lowers himself onto his elbows say BOW and treat and praise him!

5. After several repetitions you'll notice his enthusiasm. Slowly remove your hand from his belly.

6. Next, stand in front of him and do a BOW-gesture as you move your hand to the floor with a treat.

7. Phase off the treats intermittently within two weeks.

Now be creative—think of all the phrases that will be complimented by your dog's new gesture. By teaching a signal with the word you'll soon be able to prompt the reaction with a flicker of your hand while you say phrases, such as the following:

- "I am sooo tired..." (the bowing motion looks like a tired stretch too)
- "Time for bed . . . take a bow!"
- "May I have this dance?"
- "How do you do?"
- "Say hello to Grandma!"

Add more phrases to the list and teach your dog the response by signaling a bow.

TIP

Many dogs also bow down when they are excited or playful into what is known as a play bow. Practice monkey see, monkey do. Get down on your hands and knees and lean forward on your elbows. Excite your dog with a toy or by moving around in a mock play bow position until he gets excited, too. Say BOW if he copies your posture.

Dogs love to do this action whether you're asking them to or not. It provides a perfect opportunity for a belly-to-floor scratch and a good stretch.

1 Sit on the floor with your knees bent to form a tunnel. (You can also practice under objects like chairs and tables.)

2 Instruct DOWN in front of your knees.

3 With a treat, lure your dog under your legs as you say CRAWL.

4 Praise and give him a treat, adjusting your legs so that he can't stand underneath them.

5 Once your dog is catching on and crawling with delight, lure him forward on an open floor.

6 Hold your hand just above his shoulder blades and push on his pressure point if he attempts to stand.

7 Gradually introduce distance, praising and rewarding all cooperation.

This trick is an age-old favorite—for both dogs and people. Many dogs are "paw-expressive," pawing you for attention as naturally as they wag their tails. If your dog fits this description, you only need to pair the word with the behavior for your dog to make the association. If not, you can teach it easily.

1 Take your dog aside, holding a treat in your left hand. Instruct him to SIT.

2 With your right hand, tap his wrist joint gently.

3 When he lifts his paw, slide your hand underneath and say PAW as you give him the treat.

CONTINUED ON NEXT PAGE

Soon your dog will be a willing cooperator. Now you can practice some variations on the theme.

HIGH-FIVE

Gradually rotate your hand until your fingers are pointed up and your dog is slapping your open palm!

WAVE

When your dog is hitting the mark consistently, hold your hand back a few inches, and as he lifts his paw, say WAVE as you wave at him.

TIP

Want to teach wave at a distance?
First, practice in a quiet area using STAY to gain distance one foot at a time. Say WAVE as you gesture, initially praising your dog for the slightest lift of a paw. Treat and praise generously when starting out.

FAQ

My dog gets so excited when I ask for a high five, he paws me with both feet! What am I doing wrong?
Nothing, perhaps. Say HIGH FIVE in a normal tone, as he'll pick up on your excitement, and hold a hand in front of one leg to block it. Also consider a HIGH TEN!

There's no debating that dogs love to jump. To give your dog an appropriate outlet, teach him OVER and all its variations.

1 Set a broomstick over two low obstacles.

2 Take your dog to it and let him sniff it.

3 Walk back five paces and say OVER as you run with your dog on-leash and over the hurdle.

4 Continue until your dog feels safe enough to run and jump by himself.

5 Toss toys to encourage him to go over the jump alone.

6 Gradually increase the height of the jump, but do not raise it above his elbow until he is more than one year old.

Teach your dog to jump through a hoop, your arms, or a tire swing.

1. Ask a helper to hold a hoop against the broom obstacle from the OVER trick. Toss the toy through the hoop and say THROUGH instead of OVER.

2. Repeat this step until your dog feels comfortable jumping through the circle.
3. Gradually lower the broom until it lies on the floor.

4. Begin taking the hoop to various locations and saying THROUGH to direct your dog through any loop.

To teach your dog to bring things to you, do not take things away from him when he does. He will lose interest. Instead, make a big deal of praising your dog for coming back to you with the object. If you need to take the object away, give him a handful of treats or show him a more tempting substitute. For now, follow these techniques:

1 Take your dog into a small room or hallway. Toss an object and let him interact with it. Sit on the floor and cheer him on. If he comes to you, scratch his sides playfully and let him know how proud you are. Say BRING only when he is by your side.

2 Once your dog is enjoying this game and is interacting with you with the toy in his mouth, take him to a larger room or a long hallway. Toss the object and wait for him to grasp it in his mouth. Now call his name as you run away from him clapping your hands. Say BRING as he joins you, and praise him enthusiastically.

3 Begin to use the same runaway technique in larger areas, saying BRING the moment your dog grasps the object. Remember to give him a treat or exchange the object with another if you must remove it from his mouth.

Teach your dog the command GIVE. When your dog hears this command, he will spit out whatever is in his mouth. Fill a cup with treats, use a clicker to emphasize this routine when possible, and follow these steps:

1 Approach your dog while he is chewing on a toy or eating his food. Say GIVE as you approach, shaking a treat cup or pressing your clicker. Remember to offer a treat after each click. Soon, your dog will look up as you approach. Also use this technique if your dog has one of your possessions in his mouth. (See page 186 for suggestions on inappropriate chewing.)

2 Toss a toy for your dog. Approach him as he plays with it, shaking the cup or clicking.

3 Now join the directions BRING and GIVE. Start in a small room and progress to an open area. Toss a toy and run from your dog as you say BRING. When he reaches you, say GIVE as you click/treat. Phase off treating intermittently, but always praise your dog's cooperation enthusiastically.

Is your dog vocal? Teach him to do two things on cue: bark and stop barking.

1 Prompt your dog to bark. Bait him with an object, bark at him, ring the doorbell—whatever works.

2 As he barks, say SPEAK and flash a snazzy hand signal.

3 After one to three barks, say YES and offer him a treat.

4 Continue this exercise until he learns the signal.

5 Teach him SHHH! As you feed him the treat, say SHHH—GOOD.

6 Practice SPEAK and SHHH together, varying the numbers of barks between the two.

Teaching your dog to sit still may seem like an impossible task, but once he learns the commands DOWN and STAY, you're only a few lessons away from this clever trick.

1 Instruct DOWN and pat your dog gently until he's calm.

2 Scratch his ribs to get him to relax to one side.

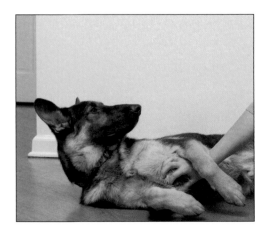

3 Gently scratch under his ears and guide his head to the floor.

4 When he is in the "dead dog" position, instruct STAY–PLAY DEAD.

5 Gradually increase the duration your dog must lie still before releasing him with OKAY and a reward and praise.

Roll Over

This trick is fun for everyone—dogs who are agile enjoy flipping over. It's fun to teach, and it's a great crowd-pleaser!

Note: *Before teaching this trick to your dog, ask yourself: Does my dog enjoy rolling onto his back? If so, proceed. If not, choose another trick to perform.*

1 Instruct DOWN and pat your dog until he rolls to one side.

2 Take a treat and guide his head over his back by drawing an invisible line from under his chin to behind his ear.

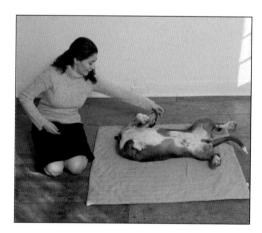

3 Help his legs over and praise him wildly for achieving the goal.

4 Continue to spot him like a gymnast until he's eagerly participating.

5 Gradually move him into a standing position, waving your arms in a motivational, sweeping signal.

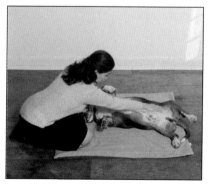

chapter **10**

The Civilized Companion

There's nothing like a well-mannered dog—fun to share and show off, she is a true pleasure to have around. Children are delighted to see and pet your dog. Doors open for you everywhere, and people learn your dog's name before they even shake your hand.

On the flip side, a poorly mannered dog is overwhelming and sad. These dogs have little impulse control and often act like bratty children desperate for attention. Although you may learn to tolerate and love your dog regardless of her bad habits, other people won't.

The potential to be a well-mannered dog lies within your dog: any dog can learn impulse control and good behavior. Her ability to succeed depends on your consistency in teaching her. If you are committed and diligent in your teaching, both you and your dog will benefit, and you'll have a lifetime of enjoyment together.

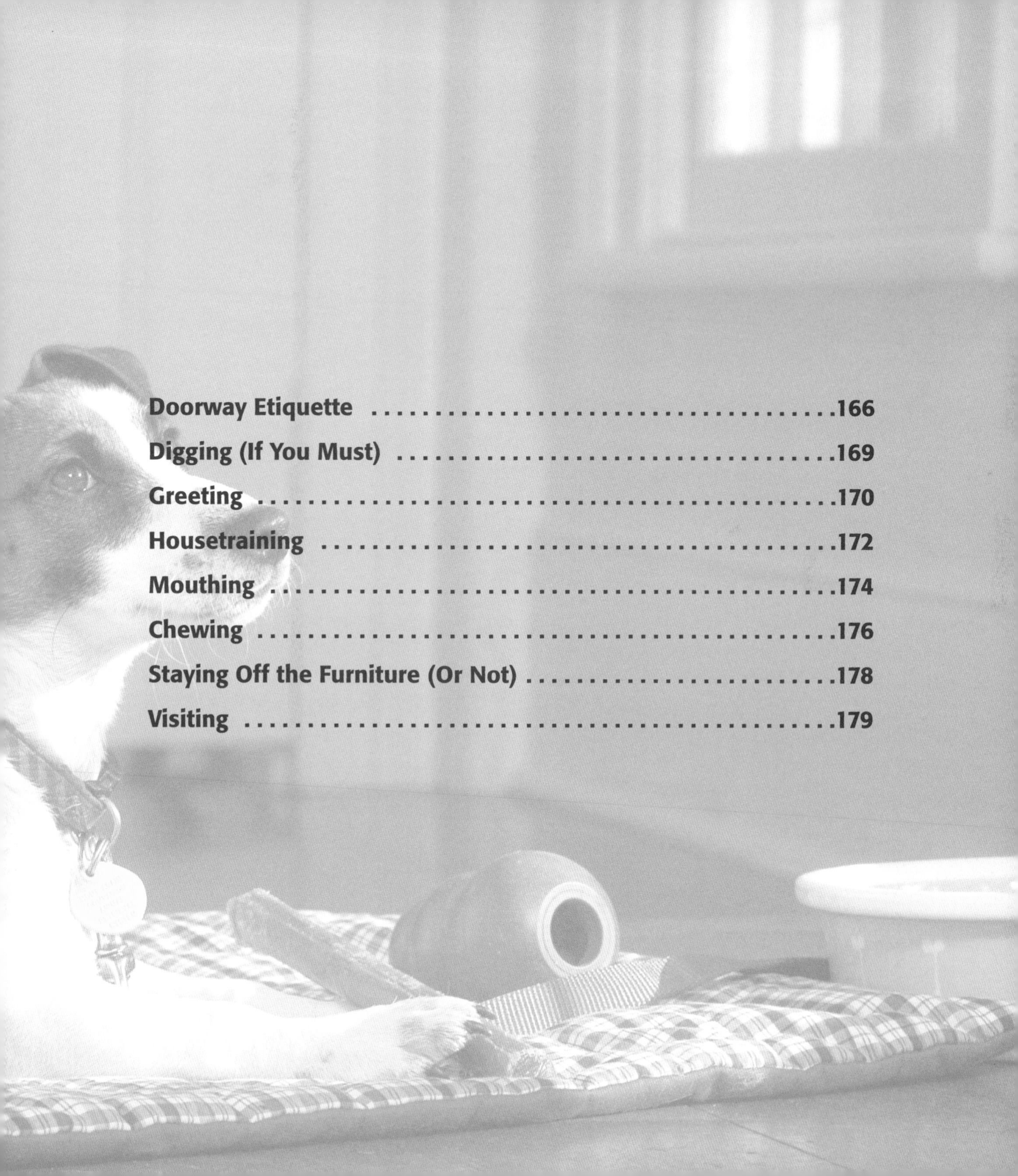

Doorway Etiquette

The doorway is where it all starts. If you let your dog barge in and out in front of you, you're communicating that she needs to be in charge. Instead, you must have your dog wait for you to lead her in and out. She will be calmer and more centered throughout the day if you do so consistently, and especially more responsive when company arrives.

When your dog is free in your home, attach a short finger lead to her collar and reinforce these exercises whenever anyone goes in or out.

Teach Your Dog WAIT-OKAY

1 Bring your dog on her training collar and leash to the threshold of a doorway. As you approach the doorway, say WAIT.

2 If she stops, praise her. If she doesn't, say NO and tug her back to your side.

3 Reinstruct WAIT, saying OKAY and leading her forward only after she has complied.

4 Go to your front door and repeat steps 1-3, both going in and coming out.

Note: If you have a fenced-in environment, there may be times when you don't need to accompany your dog out the door. In that case, instruct WAIT, pause for two to fifteen seconds, and then release her to exit on her own with OKAY.

Teach Your Dog PLACE

Your ultimate goal is for your dog to stay in your house even if the door is left wide open. This is not a hard concept for her to learn if you enforce it consistently with the following exercise:

1 Establish a "greeting station," a location five to ten feet from a door to which you can send your dog when company comes to call. You will need to secure a short leash to something immovable in this area, such as a banister, door-knob, or piece of furniture. (If there is nothing else to secure a leash to, you can always screw a metal hook to the baseboard.)

2 At a quiet time, send your dog to her selected spot, saying PLACE.

3 Secure her to the greeting station and tell her to STAY.

4 Go to the door and open it. Stand there and do not respond to any commotion. When your dog is calm, return to her and praise her quietly.

5 Repeat this process until your dog is comfortable with this exercise.

6 Progress to gradual departures. Leave the door open and go out for a minute, then two. You may stand out of sight or do a task nearby.

Do not focus on your dog when she is anxious. If you come in and she is still restless, simply stand nearby and ignore her until she calms down.

CONTINUED ON NEXT PAGE

Doorway Etiquette
(continued)

Welcome Visitors Calmly

When visitors knock or ring your bell and regardless of your dog's reaction:

1. Instruct your dog PLACE and lead her there with a short finger lead.

2. Secure her to her greeting station and tell her to STAY. Do not let her interact with or greet anyone until she has calmed down.

TIP

Is your dog voicing her protest, barking wildly when secured away from the excitement? Secure him within six to ten feet and ignore the barking. If it persists, consider a head collar or a discreet spray correction.

If your visitors are willing, ask them to close shop—fold their arms across their face—and ignore your dog until you give the green light. This body signal will transfer, and your dog will learn quickly that to get attention, she must sit.

Most dogs like to dig. Some dogs *must* dig: it's in their genetic blueprint. If they're not given an outlet, they will settle for houseplants or garden beds.

Dogs also dig when they want to hide something or when they're overheated and need to cool off. On hot days, make sure that you give your dog plenty of water, access to a house or garage, and a cool spot in which to lie.

Digging Etiquette

ESTABLISH AN ACCEPTABLE DIGGING SPOT

Before you discourage your dog from digging, select an area in which it is okay for your dog to dig. It may be on your property or in a nearby field or wooded area. Go there with your dog, say GO DIG, and dig with her. Hide treats and bones just below the surface to reinforce the lesson that digging in this spot is okay.

DISCOURAGE DIGGING

You can try several tricks to discourage digging. Place your dog's poop in holes and cover them up. You can sprinkle in some red pepper for good measure, too. If that doesn't work, try filling the hole and securing wire mesh over the top.

Avoid gardening in front of your dog. The monkey see, monkey do maxim applies to dogs, too.

Greeting

There's a civil way to greet people. Some dogs sit calmly, others do a funny trick or bring a toy, and still others roll onto their backs for a cheerful scratch. Though the delivery varies, each of these greetings has one thing in common: nobody's jumping!

Teach Civil Greetings

Dogs jump in greeting to get closer to your face. Teach your dog that sitting has the same effect. If your dog jumps when greeting you, fold your arms over your face and look up. When she calms down, brace her by looping your thumb over her collar. Pet her lovingly and teach her the meaning of SAY HELLO (to sit calmly for greeting).

When company visits, ignore your dog until she's calm. At this point, bring her to the visitors and brace her (see above) if she's excited or overwhelmed. Encourage her to sit and stay by saying SAY HELLO.

When you're out and about, many people will want to pet your dog. Decide ahead of time if your dog is comfortable greeting strangers. If so, ask the person to wait until you position your dog into a SIT and brace her (page 79) if you suspect that she will jump.

There are also etiquette rules for greeting other animals, from dogs and other small pets to horses. Having your dog lunge and drag you to a strange animal is not good form. It sets the stage for impulsivity, which, minus the leash, could put your dog in harm's way.

If you see another person approaching with a dog, tell your dog to HEEL and enforce it. If they are approaching to visit, stop, put your dog in a SIT-STAY, and wait until they are close to release her to GO PLAY. If your dog is unfriendly with other dogs, tell the person immediately to avoid any conflict.

If you are introducing your dog to another pet, determine if she will be friendly ahead of time. Small animals can trigger a dog's prey drive (an instinct to chase/kill), especially if she has not been socialized with that type of animal. Use the same HEEL, SIT-STAY combo mentioned above.

TIP

If you're approached by an off-leash dog, it's best to avoid contact. Don't look at the dog, and discourage your dog from doing so as well. Unless the dog is friendly, she may attack if she thinks you are in her territory. But by focusing on the ground and quickly moving out of her perceived area, she will save her energy for a more threatening foe.

Housetraining

Although I cover specific housetraining issues in chapter 11, I will go over basic etiquette here. Your dog can learn at a young age to take herself to a specific spot to eliminate when she has to go. You use the same philosophies as you would when potty training a child.

Go Outside to Potty

To train your dog to potty outdoors, pick an area (three feet by three feet for small dogs, five feet by five feet for larger breeds) close to your door so that your dog won't get distracted on the way to eliminate. Bring or send her to that area consistently.

1 Specify which door your dog should use to go outside, and designate a pathway to that door that everyone follows.

2 Teach your dog to indicate that she's at the door so that you'll know when she has to go. Use a bell, hung at nose level, or encourage her to bark.

3 Each time you go to the door to let her out, say OUTSIDE clearly. When your dog gets to the door, encourage SPEAK (see page 161) or tap the bell. Repeat OUTSIDE as you open the door.

4 Take your dog to the designated spot. Do not walk or interact with her: She must learn to take care of business first.

5 Stand with your dog at the area for no more than five minutes.

6 When she pees or poops, say GET BUSY once as she's eliminating, and then praise her lovingly.

7 If she doesn't go within five minutes and you're sure she has to go, bring her back inside and keep her with you on a leash, carry, or isolate her in a crate or room for fifteen minutes. Then take her out again, following the same routine.

Note: Your dog will need to go out after a bout of play, any period of isolation, a nap, or a feeding. How long after these activities varies based on her age and bladder control. Routine will tell.

Paper Training

Paper training (or wee-wee pad training) follows much the same logic as teaching a dog to eliminate outdoors. You'll need to pick one central location in a private corner near your main living space, although if you live in a large house and allow your dog to roam freely, you may need to place a few auxiliary pads in faraway rooms until she is fully trained to go in the one area.

1. Place four wee-wee pads in the designated area. Although you will eventually reduce the number to one or two pads (after two weeks, remove one pad a week until you're using only one or two), having four to start with prevents many initial mistakes and highlights the area visually.

2. If you have a large home, neatly place a couple of pads in frequented floors or wings, and use them if your dog needs to eliminate urgently.

3. Take your dog to the papers, saying PAPERS, after she comes out of her crate, she wakes from a nap, or any other time you suspect she might have to go. Do not look at, talk to, or interact with her while she sniffs the papers.

4. If she won't focus on the papers, have her wear a drag leash and stand there with her until she cooperates. If she still can't orient to the task, place the papers in a bathroom or mudroom and keep her gated until she goes.

5. As she's going to the bathroom, say GET BUSY. Praise her when she finishes.

6. If she doesn't go and you're sure that she must, isolate her or keep her with you on a leash. Take her back to her papers after fifteen minutes.

Note: Do not interact with your dog when you wake up in the morning or return home after a period of absence until after she's gone to the bathroom. Use warm, loving, calm praise to let her know how pleased you are.

Mouthing

Dogs are oral by nature. They play and interact primarily with their mouths. Watch two dogs together and you'll notice how much of their communication centers around facial and mouthing interactions.

You need to teach your dog that, despite these tendencies, she may not mouth human skin, period. This lesson is not hard to learn or to teach; it just takes consistency.

Discourage Nipping

First, teach your dog an appropriate alternative to mouthing, such as KISSES, which means licking, not biting; tongue, not teeth. Spread butter or another creamy spread on your hand and say KISSES as your dog licks it off.

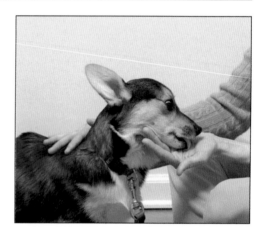

Puppies under twelve weeks are very mouthy. Do not correct soft nipping until they are older. Teach them to inhibit their bite by shouting OUCH when they bite down too hard. Remember, too, that young dogs nip to communicate needs, similar to an infant's cry. Immediately consider their needs. Puppies nip the hardest when they need to sleep, play, or poop. Address the need, not the nipping.

Also, consider the games that might be encouraging your dog to nip. Are you playing tug of war? This game encourages confrontational interaction, as does rough wrestling. Reconsider your game options; refer to chapter 9.

When your dog is mouthing you, avoid pulling your body away and/or physically correcting her. Please don't trap her mouth shut or shove your fingers down her throat, either. Doing so is both cruel and generally ineffective; when it works, it's the result of fear, not understanding.

The goal is to teach your dog spatial and body respect. Practice EXCUSE ME (see page 81) throughout the day, and leave a short lead attached to your dog's collar at all times. When she nips you, grasp the lead to pull her away from you. Then instruct SIT, and then KISSES.

If pulling her off sharply is ineffective, try the spray-away correction. Without looking at or speaking to your dog, using either product listed on page 43, discreetly spray the body part your dog is nipping so that she is unsure where the reaction came from. After she pulls away, encourage her to give KISSES.

Chewing

Dogs really enjoy chewing on objects, especially when they're young. If you don't give your dog a suitable item to satisfy this need, she will inevitably chew your belongings. This will make you frustrated, understandably, but when you convey this frustration to her, your dog won't understand you and will get even more stressed out. Dogs relieve their stress by chewing, and so the vicious cycle begins.

Encourage Appropriate Chewing

Buy several types of chew toys and see which items your dog likes the most. Although many veterinarians discourage "white" rawhide, as it can break off in chunks and expand in the belly, causing gas and indigestion, there are many other choices on the market (see page 30 for suggestions).

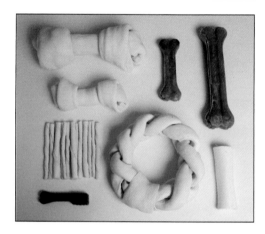

If your dog enjoys pressed rawhide, for example, buy multiples and place one at each play station. If one gets carried away, buried, or lost, physically tie it to an immovable object nearby. It will be reassuring to your dog to know that she can always find her chew in the same location.

Teach your dog a cue word like BONE. Whenever you see her acting restless or staring at you, suggest BONE, take her to her play station, and show her the bone.

If you catch your dog chewing on something that you'd rather she didn't chew, don't make a big issue about it initially. If you do, your dog will think you're challenging her for the object and may react defensively or simply learn to steal the object when you're out of sight. Many young dogs take this reaction and turn it into a game—grab-and-go!

If your dog gets aggressive, don't interact with her. Call your veterinarian and ask for a referral to a professional who can help you. Don't risk getting bitten: once a dog bites, she's far more likely to bite again.

If your dog is grabbing things when you're out of sight, you need to keep her in your sight for two weeks. Use the leading and stationing exercises described in chapter 6, and remember to yell at the tempting objects, not at your dog. In addition, spray a deterrent (see page 43) on her favorite objects and reteach the concept of NO, as outlined on pages 84–85.

If you're playing grab-and-go, you need to learn a new game: grab-and-show. Make treat cups as outlined on page 42 and spread them around your home. Place your dog on a drag lead so that you have something to step on if she darts away from you. When she takes something in her mouth, shake the cup and say WHAT DID YOU FIND? If she approaches, exchange the object for treats and say THANKS FOR SHARING. Do the same thing even if you have to corner her and step on the leash to catch her.

Staying Off the Furniture (Or Not)

Decide now whether you want your dog to be on the furniture. A puppy is oh so cuddly, but do you really want your adult dog on your lap, leaving a wake of hair and dirt? Some people don't mind it, while others do. Neither is wrong. What do *you* want?

Even if your dog is already on the furniture, you can still lay down a few simple guidelines to your cushion cuddles. Although retraining your dog will take some effort, most dogs prefer regulation to chaos.

Set Rules Regarding Furniture

You may choose a no-furniture rule, select one piece of furniture specifically for your dog, or allow her to be everywhere. If you select the last option, I recommend teaching your dog to come up only when you give her permission.

If you don't want your dog on the furniture, designate a play station (see page 39) nearby, and send her there when you're together. If she tests you by jumping up, leave her on a drag lead when she is free in the house. If she jumps on the couch, calmly approach, say NO, and send her to her station.

To teach your dog to go to a specific piece of furniture, say that word, CHAIR, for example, as you lead her to the chair. Make sure that the chair is in a central location, or she may choose you over the chair. If your dog jumps on other furniture, either instruct her to her chair or to a play station nearby.

If you plan to allow your dog on all the furniture, teach her to ask permission first. Leave her on a short leash, and when she approaches a piece of furniture, instruct SIT and WAIT. Vary the time you make her sit still before inviting her UP UP. Sometimes, deny her permission and instruct her to SETTLE on a bed instead; otherwise, she may jump on someone's lap who won't be as thrilled as you are to share the space.

Before you go visiting or vacationing, consider your dog. If she's coming with you, she'll need her own bag filled with her essentials. "Travel" is not an idea that occurs to your dog, although she would certainly rather follow you anywhere than be left at home without you.

Make Travel Fun

Pack familiar items so that your dog will feel at home in the new environment. Most importantly, take along her bedding, toys, and food.

When you arrive at your destination, set up one or more play stations for her, and sit with her there for a few minutes. Make sure that the station is in a central location so she doesn't feel left out.

While you're away from home, try to keep to your dog's regular schedule of walks and feeding. If you're going to go out without her, consider crating or isolating her in a small room while you're gone to reduce her separation anxiety.

Crisis Management

If you're experiencing frustration with your dog, you're not alone. No relationship is perfect; however, you can address a lot of problem behavior by looking at the situation as your dog would and adjusting your communication style so that your dog can better understand you. In addition, before you discourage a behavior like mouthing, you need to decide what you'd like the replacement behavior to be. If, for example, your puppy is mouthing to communicate a need to eliminate, you can teach him to ring a bell instead.

Problems are never too difficult to resolve once you look at life, and your reactions, from your dog's perspective.

Chasing

Dogs enjoy chasing things—it's instinctive and fun for them. Their early predecessor, the wolf, did it for survival.

Your dog can learn to contain his impulse to chase people, cars, and other animals, but he will need your help. Organized setups and well-defined displacement games, as described in chapter 9, will help you channel your dog's impulsiveness.

Kids

They scream, fall when pushed, and pull back when grabbed; what's not inviting about that? To teach your dog not to chase children, gather them up and decide what games they might play to help redirect your dog's enthusiasm. Surefire hits include Soda Bottle Soccer (see page 151) and Swing Toss (see page 150).

Next, practice the following exercise, with the dog on a six-foot lead and then on a retractable leash or a long line.

1 Stand just behind your dog and ask the children to enter the room and run back and forth in front of him (not around in a circle).

2 The instant your dog looks as though he's ready to chase, pull back on the leash and say NO firmly.

3️⃣ When the kids hear NO, they should freeze for three seconds. As they do, instruct your dog BACK behind your heel and praise him for complying.

4️⃣ Repeat the sequence until your dog learns to contain his impulse to chase.

5️⃣ Take the exercise outside. Practice on your six-foot lead to start, quickly progressing to standing at further distances (with a retractable leash or a long line) from him as he catches on.

CONTINUED ON NEXT PAGE

TIP

When you're working outside, you can teach your dog to play with an object instead by choosing a phrase to say as you offer him the object—GET YOUR BALL, for example.

Cats

If your dog is chasing your cat, you must first determine whether his aim is to play with or kill the cat. If it's the latter, or you can't figure it out, call a professional: you don't want to be mistaken. The telltale signs of predatory intensity include a riveted focus, ears pitched forward, a stiffened body posture, and/or an intense whine when held. Play can look similar but is usually accompanied by a playful pant and more random body postures.

If your dog is supercharged or interested in the neighbor's kitty, teach him the concept of NO (see page 83). If the cat lives with you, follow these steps:

1 Exercise your dog to near exhaustion.

2 Place him in his training leash and collar.

3 Take the cat into a small room (for example, a bathroom) and let him get acclimated to the space with a bowl of milk, perhaps, for half an hour.

4 Enter the room with your dog and watch closely for signs of elevated excitement. If you see those signs, tug the leash and tell him NO.

If the tug has little effect, try a spray-away correction. Be very discreet: he must see the correction as coming from the environment, not from you.

5 Redirect your dog with training commands and toys.

Note: *You may need to sit with the two animals in the same room for a week before you begin to notice their mutual acceptance. Gradually introduce the pair to one another in larger rooms.*

TIP

When the dog is in a main room in which the cat has previously enjoyed freedom, place the dog in an oversized playpen. In full view of the dog, shower the cat with a lot of calming attention. Over a one- to two-week period, these exercises will teach your dog to respect your cat's personal space as well as condition your cat to accept your dog's presence.

Vehicles

If your dog's chasing instinct is focused on moving targets (cars, bikes, even joggers), you need to teach him the term NO in three very defined steps:

- Inside using food and other temptations (see page 84).

- Outside using these same temptations and more irresistible lures, such as other animals, saying NO to discourage his focus and YES to praise his attention.

- In a situation in which he will face, say, a jogger, use the sidestep correction explained on page 111: note the moment your dog focuses on the jogger, step to the side, and say NO simultaneously. Encourage HEEL and praise any attention to you, however brief.

Repeat this sequence, gradually working into environments where the distractions are more prevalent.

Wild Things

Chasing other creatures is the most common form of chasing behavior: nature is banging on the door. Although you can't quash the instinct altogether, you need to make sure that you're able to control it, on- or off-leash.

Follow the same system listed for vehicles, inserting animals in the appropriate places.

TIP

If your dog is in an enclosed environment and sets out to chase a critter, let him. It will help him learn that the behavior itself is not wrong, but that there is a time and a place for everything.

Destructive Chewing

If your dog is chewing destructively, you need to examine the three *W*s.

WHY

Dogs are a purposeful species. The fact that most of their breed-specific tendencies are no longer needed, combined with the fact that our world is much faster paced than it used to be, ensures that our dogs will experience increased isolation and decreased exercise, which spells boredom. Dogs don't have the outlets that humans do to occupy their minds. Many of them chew their frustration and boredom away.

To help prevent restless chewing, increase the amount of exercise your dog gets and practice daily lessons.

WHEN

When does your dog chew? When you're at home but busy? Keep your dog with you using the Teaching Lead methodology (see page 38) and start lessons to help create an internal sense of organization and control.

Does your dog chew in front of you or out of sight? Is it happening when you're out of the house? You'll need to increase your dog's isolation in a small room, fold-out pen, or crate (left with some favorite chews) in order to teach him how to relax and to give him a proper displacement activity. Crating or securing your dog when you can't watch him does more than prevent the problem—it helps your dog learn how to be still by himself. A well-chosen bone or chew toy serves as a good displacement object.

WHAT

What is your dog's focus? If it is your objects or clothes, separation anxiety is at work; see page 198. If it is a table leg or other furniture, your dog enjoys returning to the same spot; find a bone he enjoys and tie it to the furniture for the same reliability. Just remember: everything's chewable. You'll need to keep the house picked up for a while as you condition your dog to a new chewing program.

Grab-and-Go

If your dog has a hint of the comedian in him (see page 7 for a personality description), I'm sure he's tested out this game. With a surefire attention-grabber in his mouth, he presents himself to you for a good game of chase. It's time to turn this game on its head.

If he likes to pick things up in his mouth, he'll continue to do so. You can either allow him to run, covet, and destroy, or teach him to bring over and share the objects he picks up.

Cure the Instinct to Grab-and-Go

① Make treat cups (see page 42) and place them around your home. In addition, let your dog drag a lead when you're supervising him.

② When your dog prances by, object in mouth, find a treat cup and shake it as you call to him in a positive, directive voice: BRING IT. He may look suspicious. If so, sidestep toward him and step on the lead.

③ With your foot on the lead, coax him in and treat him, while thanking him for sharing his treasure.

④ If your dog is a seasoned addict, set up a few practice situations in a small room or hallway to help earn his trust and teach him your new rules quickly.

A dog pulling on a leash is not having a good time. He's not associating going on a walk with being near you, and this could spell disaster if his leash were to break. To teach your dog to walk near you think of the leash as holding your dog's hand and find a collar that either eliminates the pulling or manages it.

USE A GENTLE LEADER

If your dog is a chronic leash-puller, review your choice of training collar immediately. If you notice a nagging cough, it's because your dog is choking, and the only thing he's learning is that being near you is asphyxiating. In this case, a "correction collar" is not the appropriate choice. Consider the Gentle Leader (see photo), which dramatically reduces your dog's resistance and can condition him over time to stop pulling you. The other options are a Good Dog collar, which gives your dog the sensation of a scruff shake with little effort of resistance from you, or a no-pull harness, which restricts his muscles' ability to lurch.

BE A TEAM CAPTAIN

Next, take your dog (in training leash and collar) to an open room or quiet area outside. Hold half the slack of the leash or tie it around your waist. Think of yourself as a team captain leading a player downfield. Call out your dog's name in a positive tone and say LET'S GO. If he lurches ahead, call his name and pivot away from him. Repeat this process over and over until either you stagger from dizziness or he starts to pay attention.

Once your dog is watching you, praise/click/treat him and work to increase the distances you can walk before turning.

PRACTICE THE HEEL COMMAND

Now practice the HEEL command (see page 88). Before each practice session, do a few quick turns to get your dog's attention.

Housetraining Difficulties

Housetraining difficulties top the human frustration chart. Dogs get confused for many reasons, and human responses add to their bafflement. Yelling at a dog or a puppy or rubbing his nose in the mess often makes matters worse. There are better ways to communicate your message.

Find the Cause

First, decide what is prompting your dog's accidents. It could be

- Illness
- Too much isolation
- Too much freedom
- Too much water
- A dominance struggle that has led to marking
- A maturity issue
- A reaction to stimuli or kenneling

Then follow this hit list:

- Take a sample of your dog's urine and stool to the veterinarian to rule out parasites or illness. If your dog seems out of sorts, take him in for a checkup.
- Measure your dog's age against the following table. If you're unable to be home and your dog needs to go out, either hire a dog walker or ask a friend to help out in your absence. If neither is available, leave your puppy in a playpen with a papered corner (see page 28).
- Restrict water to daytime hours, removing the bowl after 7:30 pm. If your dog looks thirsty at night, give him a couple of ice cubes.
- Isolate your dog in a small room or a crate when you can't be watching or leading him. Given too much freedom, he may potty on the carpet or by the door.

Potty Time	
Puppy's Age	*Number of Potty Breaks a Day*
6 to 14 weeks	eight to ten
14 to 20 weeks	six to eight
20 to 30 weeks	four to six
30 weeks to adult	three to four

CONTINUED ON NEXT PAGE

Housetraining Difficulties *(continued)*

Housetraining Schedule for Work-at-Home Owners	
Time of Day	*Potty Time*
Early morning wake up	Go outside
Breakfast	Go outside after breakfast
Mid-morning	Go outside
Afternoon feeding	Go outside after eating
Mid-afternoon	Go outside
Dinnertime (4:00 to 6:00 pm)	Go outside after dinner
7:30 pm	Remove water
Mid-evening	Go outside
Before bed	Go outside
Middle of the night	Go outside if necessary

Housebreaking Schedule for Owners Who Work Outside the Home	
Time of Day	*Potty Time*
Early morning wake up	Go outside
Breakfast	Go outside after breakfast
Lunch break feeding & walk	Go outside
Mid-afternoon	Young puppies must go out
Arrival Home	Go outside
Dinnertime (4:00 to 6:00 pm)	Go outside after dinner
7:30 pm	Remove water
Mid-evening	Go outside
Before bed	Go outside
Middle of the night	Go outside if necessary

Restrict a Small Dog's Space

Putting a small dog in any room large enough to fit a few pieces of furniture is equivalent to putting a child in a football field and asking him to hold his bladder until he makes his way across it. Small dogs need more supervision and structure initially.

Raising a Puppy?

Nothing is more exciting or frustrating at times than raising a puppy. Use the tables on the previous pages to adjust your puppy's feeding, walking, and playtimes to a structured schedule. Be gentle with your puppy; it's confusing for him, too.

Puppies experience many changes and fluctuations in their hormone levels. Your puppy may be accident-free for weeks, and then suddenly have several in a row. Don't lose faith—simply go back to the structure you had in place when you were housetraining him initially.

TIP

If your puppy has an accident, do not clean it up in front of him. Use paper towels and a neutral solution to mask the odor of his urine, which can be a trigger for another accident. For urine, step on paper towels placed over the accident until they come up clean.

Marking

If you have a dog who is marking, the issue at hand is bigger than simple confusion. Your dog believes that your home is his domain, and it is his duty to mark and protect his territory. Included in his repertoire may be protective barking, an approach-avoid display for company, or an occasional growl when he feels you're out of line. If the situation has advanced this far, ask your veterinarian to help you find a professional who can assist you in breaking this habit.

If marking is truly your only issue, try these tips:

- Isolate your dog in your home. Use a crate or the leading techniques outlined on page 82.

- Do not let your dog mark your neighborhood—he's bringing the same habit indoors. Teach him to mark outside your home, and then walk him at a HEEL around the neighborhood.

- Work on WAIT at all doors, elevators, etc. leading into and out of your home. See page 80.

Training your dog to wait at all doors will aid in your fight against marking.

FAQ

My dog is marking, all right, but he is also very nervous when away from the house and when people visit. Why is this?

Your dog is on a head trip, and you can help him. The lack of direction and structure in your home has prompted him, very much by default, to consider himself your leader. He neither looks to your direction when the environment changes nor relaxes with new people because he is not mentally equipped for this role. Marking is just another behavior that reinforces his position, though he has no interest in leading. To resolve the issue, you need to train him to watch you for direction and to listen to you when you're away from the home. Containment and supervision are necessary to curb the marking, but structure and training are a must to give him the overall sense that he can follow, not lead.

How you handle your nipping dog depends on his age. Young puppies nip to convey their needs (see page 64) and because they're curious and interactive. Older pups and dogs continue to nip in order to boss or convey rank, or because they think of their owner as more of a playmate than a leader. Techniques that encourage shoving a hand down a dog's throat or clamping the mouth shut are cruel and most dogs retaliate by becoming more aggressive or assertive in play.

Resolve Nipping

If your dog is under 12 weeks he's simply testing waters and his nips are more an indication that he's feeling needy than confrontational. Similar to a child who cries when a need is not met, a puppy will nip. His needs include hunger, thirst, play, sleep, and elimination. If you have an older puppy, he has learned that nipping is interactive and may be doing this to get attention and promote his sense of control. Try these techniques to resolve nipping:

- Teach KISSES with butter.

- Ask yourself if your puppy or dog is communicating a need.

- Stop all challenging games.

- Use the spray-away correction described on page 42 to discreetly discourage your dog from chewing on your body.

- Give yourself something to grasp by placing a drag or short lead on your dog's collar.

- Keep your hand still when your puppy or dog nips you.

- Ignore light nipping with puppies under 16 weeks of age.

- Address hard nips immediately. Let your hand go limp in his mouth, say OUCH, tug him away from you sharply, and glare into his eyes for two seconds: short and stern.

FAQ

I read that I'm suppose to hold my dog's mouth shut when he nips, but it only seems to make matters worse. What can I do?

Squeezing your dog's mouth shut is not nice. It is confrontational which would explain why he's retailiating. Stop this immediately. Bring your dog's mouth away from your hand and redirect him to another activity. If he will not relent, give him some alone time in a crate or on a station; he may be over-tired.

Jumping

If you try walking around on all fours for one day, you will have a greater appreciation for why your dog jumps up. To teach your dog not to jump, consider his motivation and meet him halfway.

To correct jumping, follow this plan:

- Be certain that your dog is getting enough exercise. See chapter 9 for appropriate games and energy outlets. Tired dogs jump less.

- Avoid confrontational games. They encourage pushing or pawing and other physical behavior.

- If your dog is jumping for attention or in greeting, close shop initially. Teach familiar company to do the same. Encourage SIT for a greeting, or the fetching of a toy. If this is ineffective, try the other corrections explained above, one at a time to determine which is most effective.

- If your dog is jumping on counters, refer to page 84 and practice the NO exercise: catch your dog when he's just *thinking* about the counter and then yell at the counter, not your dog.

- If your dog is jumping on furniture: see page 178.

Type	Reason	Alternatives
Greeting/ attention	For face-to-face interaction	SIT for attention/say hello
Counters	To see what you're focused on and to find the source of odors	SIT on mat/play with toy
Furniture	To mimic or join you; to be comfortable	Permission to join you; soft bed nearby

TIP

Instead of thinking of your dog as "bad" when he jumps, consider how interactive and connected to you he is. He watches you throughout the day: You are his hero. When you're focused on the counter or sitting on the couch, he wants to be there too!

To teach your dog the alternative behaviors, be consistent. Use one of the following corrections to convey your disapproval:

CLOSE SHOP

Fold your arms in front of your face to block eye contact. Do not relax until your dog is standing calmly on all four paws.

SIDE SWIPE

Leave a leash on your dog that you can grasp. Grasp the leash and tug your dog off to the side. The goal is to give him a feeling that's similar to slipping on ice.

REVERSE YO-YO

Let your dog drag a four-foot lead with a knot tied just beyond your dog's paws. Step on the knot when jumping is expected. Your dog will be able to get only a couple of inches off the ground before being brought back down.

SPRAY-AWAY CORRECTION

Use a spray corrector to spray a vapor boundary between his body and you/object (see page 42).

Mounting

Mounting humans is not acceptable. Ever. Mounting a toy or cushion is tolerable during a puppy's adolescence, but you shouldn't allow it to become a habit.

Stop the Mounting

Your dog/puppy is mounting for one of two reasons:

- He or she is vying for dominance in your relationship or family.
- He or she feels small and out of control.

Many times, mounting is focused on inanimate objects; it often occurs during times when the energy level in your household is escalating. If your dog mounts a pillow, either ignore it as a stage that will pass or calmly separate the two and give him a stationary command, such as SIT or DOWN and STAY.

If your dog is mounting humans, begin a training regime immediately, and involve family members and friends. Have him SIT for attention, make him WAIT at doors and for food, and teach him HEEL when you're outside and with company. If the mounting escalates to aggression, call your veterinarian for a professional referral.

Recognize that mounting is a symptom of another issue: control and dominance. You (and your family) must emphasize that you possess both: you are in control of every situation and are fully capable of being the dominant leader of your dog's family.

FAQ

My 5-month-old collie mounts our older dog constantly—a 5-year-old male collie! Is this sexual? What's he trying to communicate?

It has nothing to do with either dog's sexuality. Your puppy is restless and energetic and smart. He's also bossy. It is a passing phase, which should be ignored or gently interrupted. Assertive interruption may cause tension between the two dogs.

When you see the mounting behavior beginning to emerge, take the leash immediately, tug it as you say NO, and redirect your dog to DOWN and STAY. If your dog can't calm down, put him on a leash and bring him to your side. If you catch your dog in the act of mounting a person, calmly approach him, or grasp the leash if he's mounting you, and tug down firmly.

Next, calmly lead him to a quiet area and leave him alone for fifteen minutes.

If tugging the leash escalates the interaction, try the spray-away correction: discreetly spray down toward his feet without eyeing or shouting at him.

TIP

If a particular time or prop (a dangling leg, kids on the floor) sets the mounting in motion, be prepared. Leave a leash on your dog's training collar and correct him immediately. Corrections should be swift and firm.

Separation Anxiety

Dogs don't like separation. It takes many dogs a great deal of time to feel comfortable with being left alone. A dog who suffers true separation anxiety goes through physical withdrawal when you leave. His body temperature changes, his pulse increases, and his blood pressure rises. He acts out, not out of disrespect or spite, but out of anxiety. House soiling, destructive chewing, clawing and scratching, and barking are common reactions.

Cure Separation Anxiety

To resolve the separation anxiety issue, follow this regime:

- Train your dog twice a day. Lessons teach your dog that you're in charge and he's not. When you leave, he'll be less stressed about where you're going and why he can't come along.

- Exercise. A tired dog sleeps more.

- Isolate your dog in a small room or a crate. Pacing in a large area creates more anxiety.

- Leave him a favorite bone and toys, dim the lights, and leave on classical music.

- Exit and enter calmly. This is very important.

- Do not correct your dog after the fact, regardless of the damage. Corrections will intensify his anxiety and make matters worse.

- If you're leaving for more than six hours at a time on a regular basis, find a dog walker who can break up the day. Dogs are a social species and cannot adjust to long separations, especially when they're young.

- Do trial-run departures. Go through the motions of leaving, isolate your dog, and leave the radio on, but go out for short periods: ten minutes to start. If you come in and your dog is overly enthusiastic, ignore him until he's calm. Do this up to fifteen times in a day.

- When you're home with your dog, avoid giving him constant or unsolicited attention. Although it may relieve your guilty feelings, it is too sharp a contrast from the isolation. Instead, ask him to SIT or tell him to GET YOUR BONE.

Try not to visualize this behavior. Stool swallowers come in two varieties: those who eat their own stool and those who eat the stool of other animals. This section addresses both problems.

OWN STOOL

If your dog's eating his own stool, it's likely a compulsive behavior resulting from early puppyhood, when his mother would ingest her puppies' stool to keep the whelping box clean. Though this is probably the most grotesque thing you can imagine, in dog land it's quite normal. When your dog was a puppy, he watched his mom do it, and if and when he sees you scoop it up, he thinks, why not? To resolve this problem:

- Start a training regime immediately to help your dog focus on you and your direction, and not on his internal anxieties.

- Never clean up accidents in front of your dog.

- Do not react to your dog if he shows interest in his stool. He'll see your behavior as competition and gulp it down faster.

- If your dog's showing interest, refocus him on a favorite game: GET YOUR BALL.

- Ask your veterinarian to give you a food additive that will make his feces distasteful.

- After your dog has finished eliminating, spray the stool with something distasteful (see page 43).

OTHER CREATURES' FECES

If your dog is eating other animals' feces, it's a delicacy that borders on a human's obsession with chocolate. Unfortunately, your interference will make matters worse: your dog will see your reaction as competition and seek more and gulp faster. Most dogs outgrow this behavior if you feed them twice a day and ignore their stool fetish. Teach your dog a strong COME response as outlined on page 97. Call him to you positively and refocus him on a fun game when you notice him sniffing about.

Stimulated Peeing

If your dog tinkles during greetings, either excitedly or because he is overwhelmed, you're not alone. Certain breeds, such as Poodles and Soft-Coated Wheaten Terriers, are prone to this behavior, but there are exceptions. It will subside in time if you do the following exercises to get your dog's mind off his own tension when people arrive.

Keep Your Pup from Tinkling

- Keep your departures and arrivals low-key. Do not get excited when you arrive.

- Make treat cups and place one by the door. When you get home—and after your dog calms down—shake the cup and encourage him to do a trick (see chapter 9) or play with a toy, and then offer him a treat.

- Play a come-and-go game: Go in and out the door fifteen times in a row. Each time you return ignore your dog's hyperactivity, only reconnecting once he's calm; then use your treat cup as described above.

- Secure a greeting station as described on page 167 and place your dog there when company arrives. Ask everyone to ignore him until he calms down, and then leash him and bring him to GO SAY HELLO with a treat cup and a toy.

- If your dog is timid, ignore him. Let him relax to the situation without being approached. When your dog does approach company, have them shake a treat cup and/or kneel to pet his chest. Ask them not to make direct eye contact.

Note: If your dog does tinkle during a greeting, do not correct him. This behavior is involuntary and should be addressed as outlined here.

When your dog looks timid, your first impulse is to soothe him. Instead of reassuring him, however, your lowered posture and high-pitched voice are interpreted as fearful, only intensifying your dog's anxiety.

To help your dog overcome his fear, stand tall in front of him. Use the commands BACK and STAY to communicate authority.

Here are some tips for approaching things that might make your dog feel shy or fearful:

OBJECTS

- Approach the object confidently.
- Let your dog hang back until he feels comfortable mimicking your confidence.

PEOPLE

- Ask the person to avoid eye contact with your dog until the dog is more comfortable with the situation.
- Be friendly and calm.
- When your dog approaches, take the person's hand in yours and let your dog smell them together.
- Offer your dog a treat. (A fearful dog may or may not take it.)

GROUPS OF PEOPLE

- Let everyone know that your dog's overwhelmed.
- Instruct your dog BACK and STAY or HEEL. Communicate with him frequently, using commands to direct him and help him feel safe.

OTHER ANIMALS

- Do not force your dog to socialize.
- Tell your dog BACK and STAY or HEEL.
- Let the people accompanying the other animals know that your dog is not social with other pets. End of story. You don't like everyone you meet; don't expect it of your dog.

Correction	Environmental Correction	Tools
Leash tug	Unpleasant shift and tug	Leash, training collar when supervised
Spray-away	Mysterious vapor	Spray mister, Bianca, Direct Stop, or Bitter Apple
Noise	Alarming sound/effect	Sharp NO, penny can

TIP

If you are experiencing a level of aggression that you're unable to contain, ask your veterinarian for a referral to a reputable trainer or behaviorist in your area. Aggression is a serious signal that your dog is frustrated, and it is beyond the scope of this book.

appendix

Choosing the Right Breed

This section is ideal for those readers who have not gotten a puppy or dog and who are still considering different breeds. Although a certain breed's "look" may appeal, their personality and characteristics may not be the right match. The time spent discovering the nature of each breed, thinking long and hard about personal characteristics gives everyone involved the best chance at a harmonious future!

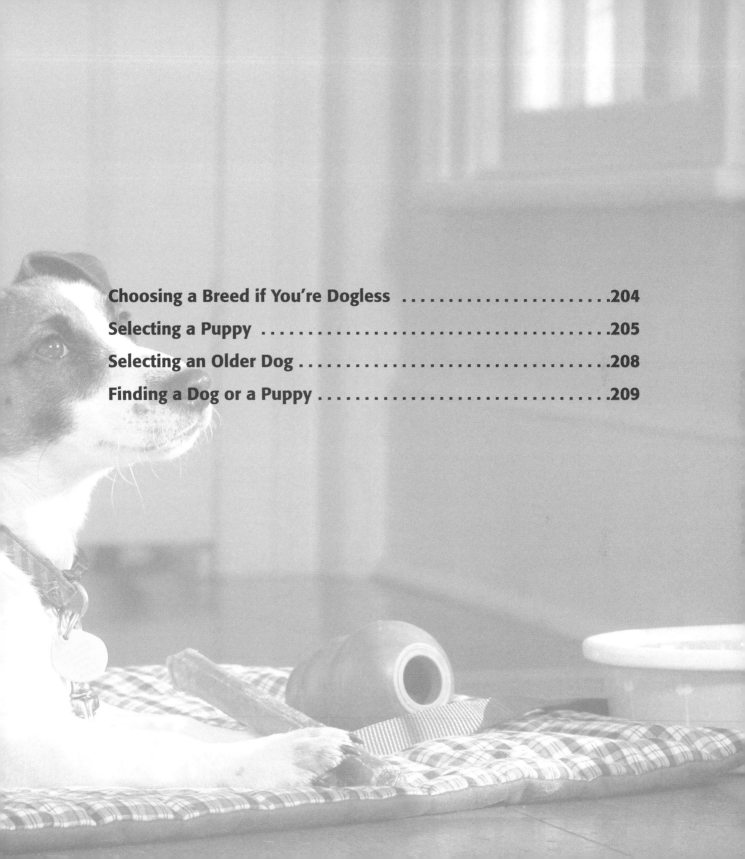

Choosing a Breed if You're Dogless

If you're thinking about adding a dog to your family, consider a suitable breed. The American Kennel Club (AKC) assigns dogs to seven breed groups: Sporting, Working, Hound, Herding, Terrier, Non-Sporting, and Toy. The groups have commonalities, yet each breed has distinct personality traits that directly reflect what the breed was originally bred to do.

SPORTING

The dogs in this group were bred to help men hunt waterfowl. Conditioned by nature to retrieve, these dogs can be trained to gather birds from the field or water, or they can simply stay at home and make excellent companions, fetching tennis balls, slippers, and the morning paper.

WORKING

Each dog in this group was bred to do a specific task, like guarding, pulling, protecting, or hunting. Serious and loyal, this group is one that needs direction and exercise to feel most content.

HOUND

These breeds like following fast-moving game, and this penchant has won them over in hunting circles. In addition to their keen noses or sharp eyesight, their easygoing and, at times, stoical personality has endeared them as family pets.

HERDING

These dogs like to herd livestock, either sheep or cattle. They are hardworking, mindful, and make wonderful companions if given direction and exercise. For these breeds the question always boils down to: Are my people sheep in need of direction or shepherds to be respected?

TERRIER

Zesty, playful, and impulsive, terriers are a determined group of dogs that was bred to hunt vermin or fight. In a home they are equally spirited and determined.

NON-SPORTING

Unlike other breed groups, there is little consistency in the personalities of these dogs because they were originally bred for different tasks. Many of these dogs, although bred for specific work, are now companion dogs as work has become hard to come by.

TOY

Many of the dogs in this group are miniaturized versions of large breeds. Too small to work, they make lovely companion dogs, although training should not be neglected as the breed instincts and group mentality is still very much alive.

MIXED BREED

The joy of owning a mixed breed is the guessing game you can play as you figure out what physical and personality characteristics come from what breed. There is a theory known as hybrid vigor that contends that mixed breeds are healthier due to a larger pool of genes.

Fill out this questionnaire as you consider what breed of dog might best suit your situation. Each question is of equal importance. Puppies are cute, but they grow up before you know it. Since many behavior traits are formed before birth, choose a puppy with desires and an energy level to match your own. You'll have between ten and fifteen years to be grateful for this decision.

The Puppy Questionnaire

1. I want a dog who
- ❑ Is naturally active.
- ❑ Enjoys quiet walks.
- ❑ Doesn't need extensive exercise.

2. As regards grooming, I
- ❑ Look forward to grooming daily.
- ❑ Will hire a professional every three to six weeks.
- ❑ Don't mind doing it a couple of times a year.
- ❑ Prefer a dog who doesn't shed.

3. My schedule
- ❑ Varies, but I'm home throughout the day.
- ❑ Requires me to work, but I will hire a dog walker.
- ❑ Is full of other activities, but I will include the dog.
- ❑ Requires my dog to be alone for stretches of time, but he will be in my thoughts.

4. I live in
- ❑ A big house.
- ❑ A small house.
- ❑ An apartment.

5. I have
- ❑ A big yard.
- ❑ A small yard.
- ❑ No yard.

CONTINUED ON NEXT PAGE

6. I am willing to commit to taking my dog to the park

- ❏ Every day.
- ❏ Four times a week.
- ❏ Twice a week.
- ❏ Never.

7. My family includes

- ❏ Children over seven.
- ❏ Children under seven.
- ❏ No children now.
- ❏ No children ever.
- ❏ Only adults.

8. My temperament is

- ❏ Exacting.
- ❏ Light-hearted.
- ❏ Laid-back.
- ❏ Concerned.
- ❏ Reserved.

9. I'd like a dog who is

- ❏ Accepting of strangers.
- ❏ Naturally protective around strangers.
- ❏ Aloof toward strangers.

10. When I go away, the dog will be

- ❏ In a kennel.
- ❏ Left at home with supervision.
- ❏ Taken along.

Interpreting the Results

1. Take a good hard look at how much time you will devote to exercising your dog. Although retrievers are an acclaimed family dog, they require a lot of exercise—pent-up energy can result in household destruction and impulsivity. If the breed you're considering cannot meet your predetermined exercise plan, pass it by!

2. Does the thought of brushing your dog's hair appeal to you? Or can you afford to hire a professional to groom your dog's coat one or more times a month? Like our hair, a dog's coat continues to grow throughout her life. If you cringe at the commitment, consider short-coated breeds, but remember—even they will need a slicking down from time to time.

3. Dogs enjoy predictability, some more than others. Consider whether the breed is companionable or dependent on human direction—that can turn into destructive neediness if you're not around. An independent breed that is more self-directed may be more content under those circumstances.

4. House size matters only if you're not committed to outdoor excursions, or if you're impartial to navigating around a human-size lump in the middle of your kitchen floor. All puppies start out small. . .

5. The measure of yard size reflects how committed you are to daily exercise. A small yard and a high-energy dog are only suitable if daily exercise is a commitment.

6. Although all dogs love adventures, some require a good run to calm down, especially during the first few years.

7. Family dynamics are as important a qualifier for breed choice as is energy level. Dogs bred to herd can get career stress in a home full of active children. Dogs with a propensity toward guarding their "catch" and food sources (terriers and hounds for example) can get nervous around young, impulsive children. When you're deciding on a breed, talk to as many knowledgeable people as you can find. (See reference section.)

8. How do you measure up? If you're an exacting personality type, having a dog who isn't concerned with human direction might be frustrating. If you're light-hearted, a dog who is very dependent on your input may be a nuisance.

9. If your house is like Grand Central Station, a protective breed won't be the right choice. If, however, the thought of having a dog who warns visitors of her presence is important to you, that would be a breed to consider.

10. Some breeds kennel well, others go on a starvation diet when taken out of their home environment. Speak to a professional about your choice ahead of time, and condition your puppy between the ages of 4 and 6 months by leaving her in this situation for a day or two.

Selecting an Older Dog

Adopting an older dog can be a lot easier than taking in a puppy. The cute factor isn't a distraction. You usually test one dog at a time, not ten. But if you have a bleeding heart, a dog's story can draw you in, even though her temperament may not be suited for your lifestyle. Nothing is sadder than rescuing an older dog and then having to return her because she doesn't mesh with your lifestyle.

Here are some things to consider ahead of time:

- Do you have children? Make sure you introduce them before bringing the dog home. Any caution or unease should immediately eliminate the dog from consideration.
- Startle the dog. Toss your keys or a can filled with pennies on the floor. Does she fall to pieces or attack them? These are not good signs.
- If you have an animal menagerie at home, make sure the dog can cope with the chaos. Ask questions and bring one of your furry pets along to test her reaction.
- Either lift the dog or ask the owner/staff member to pick her up. What happens?
- Offer her a bone or a bowl of food. Can you approach her? Any aggression is a clear warning sign.

Of course, the dog may be slightly wary of you as you are a stranger, but if you see anything extreme, back off, especially if it's aggression. Look for a dog who is accepting and shows patience with children and other animals if they are a factor.

When selecting an older dog, remember that you will probably have to deal with a few bad habits. You'll need to be understanding: bad habits are the result of not knowing what was expected of her in her last home.

You can find a dog or puppy at many places. If want a pure-bred, your best bet is getting one from a reputable breeder. Although you can find a wide range of pure-bred puppies at a pet store, their behavior may be affected for the worse. If you can resist the impulse to buy, try to wait and research a breeder with similar ethics to your own.

Mixed-breed puppies can be found at the shelter or through an ad in the paper. Here are some things to keep in mind.

AT THE BREEDER

The best breeders interact with you and ask you a lot of questions. Though it may feel like you're being interviewed, it shows that they care about the puppies. Answer honestly. Good breeders also let their puppies meet people of all ages and hear household noises (dishwasher, coffee maker, etc.). This helps the puppy get ready for life with you. Ask your breeder if she has temperament-tested her litter, and if she would mind if you met more than one puppy to determine which would be the best candidate for you.

AT THE PET STORE

If you're deliberating over getting your puppy from a pet store, here are some basic facts that are good to know:

- Pet stores do not always get their puppies from puppy mills, but many do. Ask to speak to the breeder who sent the puppy to the store. Willingness is a good sign.
- Most puppies are shipped to pet stores by bus or plane at 8 weeks and may be fearful of loud noises and big men.
- Breeders do not send the best puppies to pet stores. If you choose a puppy from a pet store, you are not doomed. Your pup has the same capacity for love. That said, avoid buying a puppy who looks sickly, acts nervous or afraid, or can't calm down after half an hour of interaction.

AT THE SHELTER

Getting a dog from a shelter is a noble act, but prepare yourself for what can be a sad experience. Decide ahead of time the age range you're looking for and call to see if the shelter has a dog to fit that description. When you go to the shelter, speak to the staff and let them know what physical and personality traits you're looking for—they often know each dog well and can guide you to a dog who fits your description. Here are some other things to do:

1. Find out your candidate's history. If the dog has been abused or neglected, he'll have behavior problems that you'll need to be prepared to work with.
2. If you have or plan to have children or other pets, determine if the dog likes them before bringing him home.
3. Ask about the dog's health. Are there any conditions you should know about?
4. Walk the dog. Try to brush her. Feed her treats. Give her a toy: can you take it from her or does she protect it? If she won't release it or if she growls at you, don't get that dog. These are signs of dominance and aggression that may get worse without professional help.

FAQ

What is the best age to bring a dog home?
The best age to bring a dog home depends on one thing: whether you're getting a dog or a puppy. A puppy should come home between 8 and12 weeks. If you're getting a dog, you may have a few behavior problems to correct; younger is better.

appendix B

Finding the Right Professionals

From your dog's doctor to dog walkers, it will take an experienced strong staff of professionals to meet your dog's needs and to put your mind to rest. Take some time now to line up the right group, looking into stores, kennels, interviewing dog walkers and veterinarians to ensure you've got a team that you feel comfortable with.

Choosing a Veterinarian

Find a veterinarian you feel comfortable with—someone who will discuss all your concerns and questions. You can start looking for a veterinarian before you bring your dog home, or if you are not satisfied with your current choice, interview others.

Talk to other dog owners or friends about their experiences. Call and ask if you can stop in to see each facility. Veterinarians are busy, so they may or may not have time to meet you, but you can talk to the staff. Here are some good questions to ask:

1. How many doctors are on staff?

2. Is someone on call after hours, or do they recommend a twenty-four-hour clinic? (Keep this number by your phone in case of emergency.)

3. Do they have any handouts or reading that they suggest in preparation for your dog's/puppy's arrival?

4. Can you bring the dog in before his appointment to give him a positive experience?

5. What is their recommended vaccination schedule? It will be more frequent with a puppy than an older dog, but older dogs also need visits to test for heartworm and get vaccine boosters.

Once you are happy with your selection, try to stick to one doctor. Not only will this person get to know your dog, but your dog will form a relationship with him or her as well!

There are times you will need to ask other people for advice and help. Of course, there is as much advice about how to raise a dog or a puppy as there is on raising children. Avoid testing out different theories on your dog, you will only confuse him. It's best to seek out professional advice when you need help with your dog, and to find other people who may help you with your dog's everyday needs, from feeding to exercise.

PET STORE PROFESSIONALS

Locate a reputable pet store with staff that are aware of their inventory. Ask them if they know your breed or describe your dog's temperament (bring your dog along if that is an option) so that they may better assist you in the selection of diet, toys, collars, and leashes. Try to develop a relationship with the staff so that you can speak with them about important issues. and ask for advice throughout your dog's life.

DOG WALKERS

Having someone to step in and play with or walk your dog when you can't is invaluable, especially if you are housetraining your dog/puppy. If you are working during the day, you may rely on this person a lot. Find several names if you can and interview each. These are people who will be in your house and who will be handling your dog when you are not there to watch. Here's a check list:

- Does he have a rapport with your dog?
- Are you comfortable with this person in your home?
- Get references and check them.
- How long has he been in business? How long has he lived in the area?
- How long will he spend with your dog each visit?

A good, reliable dog walker can get very busy, especially around the holidays. Does the individual have backup when he gets busy? If so, meet and check the credentials of that person, too.

Set up a system that allows you to check the activities of each visit. A simple check-off sheet allows you to know that he did come and what happened during his visit.

- Did my dog eat his food?
- Pee-pee? Poops?
- How long did you walk/play?

CONTINUED ON NEXT PAGE

HOUSESITTERS

If you travel, you may want to consider having an individual stay at your home while you're away. This person can take care of your dog/puppy as well as your home and garden. When interviewing, ask the same questions listed above and check ALL references. If you are working on a specific training program or using commands, write them down so that this person can follow the same routine and plan.

GROOMERS

Put some thought into just "who" and "where" you will take your dog to be groomed. You'll be relieved when you have to leave him behind for the day.

Most dogs are less than thrilled at spending a day at the beauty parlor: find somewhere welcoming and clean, with handlers who care for your dog as much as you do. Here's a quick check list.

- Is the floor clean? Ask to see the room where you're dog will be clipped as well as where he'll wait his turn and/or dry after bathing.
- Speak to the front staff and the groomers with your dog at your side. Do they make you feel welcome? How do they respond to him?
- Ask to see photo options for a particular cut: buzz, puppy cut, or show style. Your dog can come out looking very different.
- What are their policies for pick up, drop off and payment?

KENNEL

Another option if you travel is to kennel your dog. Kennels have limited space and can get crowded around the holidays so plan ahead. Visit the various kennels in your area to determine which you feel most comfortable with. Here are questions to ask and things to watch out for:

- Is the environment clean?
- Are the staff people and those who will care for your dog friendly?
- Will they show you the runs?
- Can you leave your dog with familiar toys or bedding? (If so, label the bedding with your dog's name/run number.)
- What do you have to pay extra for? Things that incur extra expense may include bringing your own food rather than using theirs, extra walks and personal interaction, grooming activities, and administering medication. These items can add up, so check ahead of time.

Some dogs enjoy a kennel environment while others get stressed. If you can, leave your dog/puppy for a few short stays to get him more comfortable with this chaotic environment.

DOGGY DAY CARE

You can also take your dog/puppy to a day care facility that is specifically suited to stimulate, nurture, and exercise your dog during the day. It is a great option if you are gone from home for long hours or if you feel that your dog will benefit from the socialization and exercise. To see if there is a facility in your area, call your veterinarian or speak to the people at a local pet store. Use the same list mentioned in the "Kennel" section to determine if it is a healthy environment in which to leave your dog.

FAQ

Day care sounds too good to be true. Do the dogs ever fight? What are the downsides?

These are important questions. Ask each facility what policies it has in place, how it prevents confrontations, and how it separates dogs (for example, according to size and age).

A downside to day care is that your dog may come back exhausted. Some dogs also get a bit sassy and may ignore your direction, whereas before they looked to you for direction in new situations. It's not a huge problem, and it's one that an extra dose of training can overcome. If your dog is too tired to interact with you, limit the number of days you take him to day care or consider a dog walker instead.

Everyday Care and Concerns

Your dog is neither image conscious nor able to take care of her personal hygiene. She needs your help in those departments. From clipping her nails to checking her skin, it's all up to you.

The time commitment required for brushing depends on the type of dog you have and how often she sheds. Dogs shed year-round, twice a year, or not at all. Here we describe the types of brushes available, and their functions.

Make every effort to make brushing a positive experience—use treats or a creamy spread like peanut butter to encourage cooperation. Brush your dog as she enjoys her treats. Make it a special time—go into a quiet room to help her feel calm and relaxed.

The type of brush you use is also a consideration. Wire bristles, especially when used on young puppies, hurt and create a negative association with being brushed. A common scenario is a puppy who mouths the brush or hand because she feels discomfort, only to be disciplined. Needless to say, she will hate being brushed in the future. Work hard to create a positive experience. Here's a list of different types of brushes and what types of coats each is best used for:

WIRE-BRISTLE BRUSH

A wire-bristle brush that removes hair and dirt.

SOFT-BRISTLED BRUSH

A soft brush that is especially good for puppies.

GROOMING RAKE

A short-toothed comb that is ideal for breeds with short or double coats, such as Siberian Huskies and Newfoundlands.

STRIPPING COMB

A comb that strips both undercoat and dead hair as well as smooths and flattens a dog's coat. It is frequently used with wire-haired breeds.

DEMATTING COMB

This comb prevents matting and losing coat length. It is ideal for non-shedding dogs with "hair," and dogs with a feather coat.

SHED BLADE

Good for short-coated breeds, especially when they are shedding.

FLEA COMB

A comb with small teeth that removes fleas and ticks. It can be used on all coats, provided the coat is mat-free.

Nail clipping and bathing are important to your dog's overall health and hygiene.

Clip Your Dog's Nails

Your dog's nails grow continuously. To prevent scratches or splitting (which may lead to infection), you need to clip them or take your dog to a groomer or veterinarian to have them clipped.

If you plan to do this job yourself, learn to do it properly so that you avoid clipping into your dog's nail bed. Clipping this fleshy area is similar to clipping off the tip of your finger. Bleeding will be profuse, and the wound will hurt.

To clip your dog's nails, buy a quality clipper at your local pet store. It looks like a miniature hand-held guillotine. (This is not a child's toy. Do not let children handle the nail clipper.) Ask the pet store professional for instructions if she seems competent.

It's best to clip your dog's nails before they become long and irritating. One way to tell whether it's time to trim is to listen to your dog walk across an uncarpeted floor. Can you hear her nails clicking? They're too long. Time for a trim.

Clipping your dog's nails regularly will help make the task repetitive and simple. You'll need to clip off only the tip of the nail, at the point where it starts to curl. Your job will be easier if your dog has light-colored nails, as you can easily see where the nail bed begins.

Choose a quiet time to do this task, when your dog is restful and calm. Let your dog sniff the clipper, and open and shut it several times as you give her treats to get her accustomed to the sound. Use a creamy spread or a favorite bone to keep your dog distracted as you cut her nails.

Front nails grow faster than back ones, so start there. Only do as many at one time as you can calmly. If your dog is fussy, handle her paws throughout the day as you give treats and praise her.

Purchase styptic powder from the pharmacy to use if you clip into your dog's toe by accident. It helps stop the bleeding.

Bathe Your Dog

To bathe your dog, gather her toys and a creamy spread to rub onto the side of the bathtub. Also put a towel on the bottom of the basin so that she feels comfortable standing. The calmer she feels, the easier it will be to bathe her.

Brush your dog before you bathe her: Doing so prevents knots and excessive shedding. After you're done, cheerfully lead her to the bathing area on-leash to prevent any chaos. Although she may be reluctant initially, be as positive and calm as possible. If you get upset, you'll only make matters worse.

The best soap to use is gentle baby soap or a shampoo made for dogs. Speak to a local pet store professional or a groomer.

TIP

Think ahead! Use a command like BATH TIME and get your dog used to being led to the area when she hears this phrase. Do not put her into the water until she follows you cheerfully. When you first put her in the basin, just wet her legs—don't use soap. After she accepts this, you can try a full bath. Always use treats and toys to boost her enthusiasm.

Teeth, Eyes, and Ears

Clean your dog's teeth regularly and monitor her eyes and ears for signs of illness or infection.

Clean Your Dog's Teeth

Dogs can get plaque buildup and gum disease just like humans. One way to prevent this problem is to brush your dog's teeth. To do so, purchase a specifically formulated toothpaste and toothbrush.

1. Introduce the toothbrush. Rub it in some meat juice to make the first association pleasant.
2. When your dog accepts this new activity, put just a little of the paste on the brush. Most dogs enjoy the flavor. Brush front to back and then up and down.

Note: As your dog ages, watch for signs of gum disease or tooth decay. The most telling sign is bad breath. Other signs include plaque buildup and swollen or red gums.

Check Your Dog's Eyes

Your dog does not see as sharply as you do and cannot distinguish color. She does, however, have night vision that can help her see shapes more clearly and navigate in the dark. To ensure your dog's eyes are healthy, notice what they look like when she is well. There should be no discharge, and they should be bright and clear.

Your dog has a third eyelid to protect her eyeball from dust and dirt. This lid is susceptible to infections like conjunctivitis; if you notice excessive tearing or wincing, take her to the doctor immediately. Eye infections can be highly contagious, so keep her home until the veterinarian says it's okay.

Note: Chronic tearing that leads to hair discoloration is common in many toy and hairy breeds. Ask your groomer's advice and feed your dog curly parsley with her meal to limit the discoloration.

Clean Your Dog's Ears

A dog's hearing is very good—far better than a human's. Your dog relies heavily on her sense of hearing, and you must check her ears to ensure that they are clean and free of infection. Dogs with floppy ears are more susceptible to ear infections as their ear cavities are closed off. Wipe your dog's ears out monthly, or ask a specialist to help you. If there is excessive wax buildup, your dog may have an ear infection, which can result in swelling, fever, and an imbalance if not treated immediately.

WIPE YOUR DOG'S EARS

1. Wrap your finger in a cotton pad and dip it in commercial cleanser.
2. Swab the ear thoroughly.
3. Continue with fresh pads until one comes out clean.
4. Clean the skin on the inside flap.

If there is a lot of brown waxy goop, bring your dog to the veterinarian: it is likely that she has an ear infection. If she does, you'll be given eardrops to give your dog daily. Use a treat or peanut butter to distract and please her while you are giving the drops.

In addition to regular grooming, you should check your dog for lumps and bumps that may not be readily visible to the naked eye. You should also know how to take your dog's temperature and how to administer medicine to your dog. These important healthcare checks and techniques are described below.

Examine Lumps and Bumps

Give your dog a full body petting each day. It will allow you to notice any unusual lumps, bumps, or skin irritations. There are conditions that are temporary such as a scrape from a branch, a bite, or a fatty tumor; and other irritations that may get worse such as cancer or hematomas. Keep an eye on the area and call your veterinarian if it gets worse or does not go away. Here are a list of common skin irritations and swelling:

1. Fatty tumors
2. Cysts
3. Warts
4. Bug bites
5. Hematomas
6. Tender knots (following injections)
7. Tumors (cancerous formations that may be benign or malignant)
   a. Skin cancer
   b. Bone tumor
   c. Mast cell tumor
   d. Cell carcinoma
   e. Melanoma
   f. Reproductive tract tumors

Always be on the lookout for growths and skin irritations that do not heal within a week. Speak with your veterinarian and follow her recommendations.

Take Your Dog's Temperature

There are no sweat glands on the nose, so it is a good predictor of body temperature. Ideally, the nose should be cool and wet. If it is warm or hot, your dog may have a fever. The fever is her body's way of trying to rid itself of an infection. You can also feel the other parts of your dog's body without fur (inside the ears, the belly, and pads of their paws) to see if they feel hot too. If they don't become cooler within twelve hours, you can take your dog's temperature with a rectal or underarm thermometer. The normal body temperature for a dog is 101.5 degrees (plus or minus a half of a degree). Call your veterinarian if there is no improvement or if you suspect another illness, such as Lyme disease or parvovirus.

CONTINUED ON NEXT PAGE

Medicate Your Dog

1. Let your dog smell the bottle before attempting to use it.

2. Give your dog a treat or peanut butter to pleasantly distract her.

3. Kneel down behind your dog and cradle her between your legs, petting her and giving her treats until she is calm.

4. Slowly lift your arms from the floor to the area you're medicating. Again, give her treats or peanut butter to ensure cooperation.

5. Medicate her as you tell her she's a good dog.

6. Never discipline your dog for being afraid. This may cause a fear-based aggressive reaction.

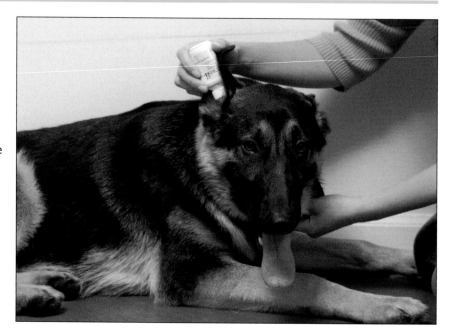

FAQ

When should I call the veterinarian?

If there is any change in your dog's behavior, including exhaustion; a persistent hot nose; swelling; whining, limping, or wincing in pain; sudden aggression toward you; a growth or an irritation that does not go away or that increases; a persistent odor; eye, mouth, or nose discharge; recurring vomiting; bleeding from the mouth or the bottom; or bleeding that is excessive, call your veterinarian.

In the case of an emergency, call your veterinarian immediately, and have an emergency animal hospital number on hand in case of an off-hours need.

If you have a female dog, you will have the choice to spay her to prevent her from having puppies. This surgical procedure removes her ovaries. It requires that your dog be anesthetized; recovery takes five to ten days.

A male dog is neutered. This procedure also requires anesthesia, although it is a much simpler operation as the testicles are removed once they have descended from the dog's body.

Things to Consider

WHY YOU SHOULD CONSIDER SPAYING OR NEUTERING YOUR PET

I strongly advocate these procedures if you do not intended to breed your dog. Breeding is a serious commitment and can lead to fatal complications. Dogs who remain sexually viable fight; roam more; mark often (pee inside in several areas); and are far more susceptible to health risks, including breast, ovarian, uterine, and cervical cancer for female dogs and testicular cancer and prostate infection for males.

WHEN SHOULD YOU SPAY OR NEUTER?

Opinion varies. Speak to your veterinarian. Standard philosophy recommends between 6 and 8 months. For a female, it is best to spay before she goes into her first heat cycle. A heat cycle indicates that the dog is receptive to mating and can get pregnant. This can occur between 7 and 12 months.

Dietary Decisions

What you feed your dog can affect her behavior; the size, smell, and volume of her stools; and the speed of her growth. All foods have a balance of protein, carbohydrates, fats, vitamins, and minerals, and you should consider the percentage and ingredients used in each category. If you need further help deciphering dog food labels, ask your veterinarian or pet store professional to help you make sense of them.

Dog Food Examined

Ask a knowledgeable person, either in a pet store or at a vet clinic, to help you decipher the list of ingredients. Protein sources can vary—it is best to choose a food that uses meat or animal protein over vegetable or grain proteins, which can cause large, odorous stools.

- Protein (21–26 percent): Protein gives your dog energy. It also helps regulate her temperature and stress. If your dog exercises a lot, she'll use more protein.

- Carbohydrates (42 percent): Carbohydrates provide your dog with a complex source of energy. Find out which carbohydrate is used to meet this requirement. Corn is cheap, but it can also cause indigestion and allergic reactions. Choose a brand that mixes other vegetables and grains into the diet.

- Fats (15–20 percent): Fats provide your dog with a shiny coat and make digestion run smoothly. Fats are the most costly ingredient in pet food as they don't store well at normal temperature. Cheap fats include the same ingredients that go into making candles, but these fats cannot be digested and don't help your dog look or feel her best. Poor-quality fats also can lead to gas. Positive fats include chicken fat, safflower oil, and canola oil.

- Vitamins (1 percent): Vitamins are necessary to unlock the nutrients in food. Supplementation may be recommended: speak to your veterinarian. Vitamins A, B, C D, E, and K are daily essentials.

- Minerals (1 percent): Minerals also help your dog with daily functioning, including circulation and energy production. Do not supplement your dog's diet unless instructed by your veterinarian: having too many minerals can be harmful.

The chief difference between dry and wet food is the water weight and shipping cost. No study has proven that one is better than the other. Some veterinarians recommend mixing the two.

CANNED FOOD

Most commercial canned food is filled with 75 percent water, so if you choose this diet, follow instructions or ask your veterinarian how much you should feed your dog. Grocery store canned food is often filled with strong-smelling meatlike contents that in actuality may not be a healthy choice. Chemicals are used to create both the coloring and the smell of the food. A better alternative is to visit a reputable pet store and select a higher-quality canned food made with natural ingredients.

SEMIMOIST FOOD

Most semimoist foods are filled with a lot of chemicals to give them the appearance and the color of meat. Although this food is enjoyed by dogs, it is not a good-quality diet. Smelly, loose stools are often the result.

DRY KIBBLE

Dry kibble is a lot like cereal. Each one looks similar, so let the ingredients and the percentage of various nutrients be your guide. With few exceptions, you get what you pay for: a high-quality dry food has human grade ingredients, and in the end, your dog will be healthier both mentally and physically for it. Speak to a pet store professional about your options.

Dry food requires careful storage. If you let it sit around too long, the vitamins may start to go bad, and the bag may attract mold. Store dry dog food in a sealed container.

TIP

If you want to change your dog's diet, do it gradually. A fast change can cause serious stomach upset. Follow this schedule over a six-day period.

Days one and two	¼ new, ¾ old
Days three and four	½ new, ½ old
Days five and six	¾ new, ¼ old

If your dog continues to have trouble assimilating to her new diet, speak with your veterinarian.

appendix D

Kids and Dogs—from Coming Home to Everyday Living

Whether you're expecting your first child or you're trying to balance the activities and schedules of many, this section covers how to organize and arrange your schedule so that everyone—from your smallest child to your dog, feels included.

Preparing for a New Baby

Expecting a baby? You've got a lot to look forward to—and a lot to get ready for. Don't leave your dog out of the loop. He'll have his own interpretation of the new bundle, and there is plenty you can do now to ensure a favorable first impression.

BEFORE BRINGING BABY HOME

There are a few secrets to helping your dog adjust to sharing your love with a baby. Start carrying a baby doll around with you and do all the daily essentials that the new baby will require. If you can find a tape recording of a baby's cry, get it, or ask a friend to make one for you. Work hard on your containment skills, STAY and WAIT, and teach your dog to stay off the furniture now. If you're anticipating increased isolation for your dog, get him accustomed to that ahead of time as well. If you wait, he may see the baby as limiting his freedom.

SET STRUCTURE IN ADVANCE

Think ahead to places you will sit to feed your baby. Your baby will be fragile and small: teach your dog to lie on the floor next to you, not in your lap.

Your dog will want to be a part of all the new activities—yes, even the dirtiest diaper change. Organizing this event in advance will make the transition smoother.

Going down the stairs with a newborn can be scary. Don't let your dog vie for stair space. Teach him to WAIT at both the top and the bottom of the stairs to avoid mishaps.

If your kitchen wasn't the hub of your existence before, it will be now. Teach your dog to lie in one corner or just outside the door.

HOSPITAL SEPARATION

When you race off to the hospital, your thoughts will be far from home. Your dog, however, will miss you tremendously and be confused by the sudden change in energy and schedules. Have someone bring a hospital rag home with your and your baby's scent on it to help him recognize the new addition when you come home for the first time.

TIP

Teach your dog hand signals to go with your commands as directed on page 95. You'll rely on them more than you can imagine.

ARRIVING WITH YOUR BABY

Ask a family member or a friend to go to the house before you get home to exercise your dog. Ask them to leash your dog when you arrive so that you may use the leash to control his enthusiasm. Leave your baby in the car seat and wait until your dog calms down completely before introducing them to one another.

If your dog is rowdy, secure his leash to an immovable object, or stand on the leash to prevent a jumping incident.

Use treats to focus your dog. Each time he approaches the baby, instruct a SIT or DOWN and reward him.

Place leashes around the house for easy access when you need to quickly control your dog's activity.

HANDLE VISITORS

Your home will suddenly become very popular. Visitors will stop by, enthusiastic to get a peek at your baby. If this is your first child, your dog will be confused by the lack of attention.

Buy some special toys/bones to give your dog when people arrive. Teach your dog to SIT and WAIT, and secure him to a nearby station lead if he can't control his excitement.

HELP YOUR DOG ADAPT TO A NEW SCHEDULE

Until you have a child, you can't imagine how much your schedule will change. And if you are not settled with just one child the demands on your time to increase exponentially as you increase your brood.

Your dog's biological clock won't change, and his daily needs will remain very much intact. He will still get hungry, have to eliminate, and need to play. Although it is understandable that you will forget even your own hygiene, your dog may act out if you forget about him.

If possible, ask a neighbor, a friend, or a family member to step in and take over any or all of your dog-parenting roles, and to fill in as playmate, nurturer, and dog walker. Your dog will be less mystified by the new addition and may take the extra attention to mean that the baby is a magical, not a threatening presence.

Kids and Dogs

To have the most fun raising children and dogs together, you need to stay positive. Children like to be involved with fun projects. To make raising and training your dog fun, use interactive charts and motivational incentives, such as TV, chocolate, or money, to encourage your children's participation.

Flip Negatives to Positives

It is easy to get frustrated or angry at a dog or a child, and sometimes a mix of the two can be overwhelming. Plan ahead of time and make a list of activities you can use as an alternative to yelling at either one of them.

- Close shop (cross your arms over your face and look up) instead of saying, "Don't push the dog when he jumps."
- Teach KISSES with butter instead of getting angry at perpetual nipping.
- Use treat cups and games to motivate your children's participation in lessons versus pinning them down to a fixed schedule.
- Also, have them help create play stations, with mats and toys, and fun charts that include special incentives.

Time	Activity	Sunday	Monday	Tuesday	Wednesday	Thursday	Friday	Saturday
	Daily Doggie Activity Chart							
7:00 am	Out							
7:15	Feed and water							
7:30	Out and play							
8:00–11:30	Lead, station or crate, and supervised freedom							
11:30	Out and play							
12:00 pm	Feed and water							
12:15	Out and play							
12:30–3:30	Lead, station or crate, and/or supervised freedom							
3:30	Out and play, explore							
4:00	Feed and water							
4:15	Out							
4:30–7:00	Lead, station or crate, and supervised freedom							
7:00–9:00	Family interaction							

Model Credits

We offer our heartfelt thanks to all the dogs and their humans who served as models for the photos in this book. Special thanks to Janet Spina, owner of Diva and Jasper, who are not pictured here. Other contributors include the following:

Thomas and Lily Arnell with Rocket, Liberty, and Rudy

Julianne, Melissa, Grant, and Allison Beck with Charlie

Doreen Blanco with Chloe

Ross Burbank with Rocky

Sarah and Jake Chintz with Monroe

Sonya Cruz with Dallas

Terri Goldsmith with Skyler

Hans Hallundbaek with Faith

Kimmarie Hornbeck with Bayli

Jessica Kappus with Kody

Lydia Landesberg with Ace

Rosemary Lee with Eugene, Charlie, and Lucy

Denis Lloyd with Duffy

Conor McSpedon with Monty and Marta

Sheila McSpedon with Monty and Marta

Melissa Miller with Benny

Jenna Rose, Devon, and Brett Novick with Nikki

Rebecca Reid with Willie

Pamela Smith with Bella

Sandra Sterling with Bob

Ben and Jared Torres with Maizy

Christina Zacharia with Finnegan

Index

A

adult dogs
- furniture privileges, 67
- locating, 209
- personality testing, 6–7
- point training, 86–87
- selection considerations, 208

ages, puppy/new home introduction guidelines, 209
aggression, 50–53
alpha pair, pack theory, 12
American Kennel Club (AKC), breed groups, 204
animals (other). *See also* wildlife
- greeting etiquette, 171
- socialization introduction, 138–139
- timidity controls, 201

animal shelters, puppy/dog source, 209
appliances, household sound conditioning, 60
attention. *See also* focus
- behavior motivation, 13
- clicker training, 44–45
- off leash walking importance, 110–111
- polite puppy requests, 71

Attention Scale, behaviors, 13
attentive (eager to please), personality type, 4
automobiles, 35, 37, 40

B

baby gates, 28
BACK command, 183, 201
barking behavior, 19, 42–43
baths, grooming element, 219
BATH TIME command, baths, 219
beds, home/travel guidelines, 29
behaviors
- Attention Scale, 13
- cause/effect guidelines, 24–25
- children's interaction, 54–57
- default recognition, 127
- distraction/displacement techniques, 73
- EP, EP command discouragement, 72
- motivation factors, 13
- NO command response concepts, 83–85
- polite puppy requests, 71
- puppy encouragement vocalizations, 65
- sleep interruption reactions, 53

behavior traits, pack leader, 12
bells, housetraining uses, 41
belly, leadership exercises, 49
biting behavior, 25, 35
Bitter Apple, undesirable behavior adjustments, 43
boarding kennels, desirable traits, 214
body language, 19–21. *See also* communications; postures
body language (yours), communication element, 17
bonding, 52, 98, 115
BONE command, 81, 176
bossy (strong-willed), personality type, 4
bows, trick training, 153
breath spray, undesirable behavior adjustments, 43
breeders, puppy/adult dog source, 209
breeds, AKC (American Kennel Club) groups, 204
BRING command, object retrieval, 159

brushes, 218
bumps, healthcare check, 221

C

canned foods, dietary guidelines, 225
cargo leads, automobile travel, 37
catch me behavior, object retrieval, 25
cats, chasing behavior discouragement, 184
chain collars, training guidelines, 32
chasing behavior, control techniques, 139, 182–185
check chains, training collar, 32
chewing behavior
- appropriate object encouragement, 176–178
- control techniques, 186
- NO command concepts, 84
- spray-away shooters, 42–43

chew toys, 30, 73
children
- activity schedules, 230–231
- behavior training, 54–57
- chasing behavior discouragement, 182–183
- conditioning guidelines, 57
- face-to-face encounters, 54
- impulsivity reaction training, 55
- new baby preparation, 228–229
- play activity reaction, 25
- positive attitude, 230
- posture guidelines, 17
- predatory reaction behavior, 54
- socialization training, 131
- touch reactions, 56
- toy competition, 55
- vocal tone reactions, 56

Chow Chows, tail/rear touching, 49
citronella, undesirable behavior adjustments, 43
classes, training, 9
clicker training, 44–45
close shop correction, jumping behavior, 195
coats, grooming, 218
collars
- fit measurements, 31, 32
- identification tags, 31
- puppy introduction, 68–69
- training types, 32–33

combs, 218
COME command
- alternative cues, 117
- bonding reconnection, 98
- clicker training, 44
- hand-feeding techniques, 52
- name associations, 97, 115
- off leash walking, 115–119
- outdoor drag leads, 35
- overuse, 117
- reconnection, 115
- response reactions, 118–119
- separation distance, 99–100, 115
- teaching techniques, 97–100
- trust building, 116
- vocal tones, 97

comedian, 4, 187

Want instruction in other topics?

Check out these
All designed for visual learners—just like you!